The
Elements
of
Playwriting

Second Edition

The
Elements
of
Playwriting

Second Edition

Louis E. Catron
late of the College of William and Mary

Norman A. Bert
Texas Tech University

WAVELAND

PRESS, INC.

Long Grove, Illinois

For information about this book, contact:
Waveland Press, Inc.
4180 IL Route 83, Suite 101
Long Grove, IL 60047-9580
(847) 634-0081
info@waveland.com
www.waveland.com

10-digit ISBN 1-4786-3597-5
13-digit ISBN 978-1-4786-3597-0

Printed in the United States of America

7   6   5   4   3   2   1

Contents

Preface to the Second Edition

Updating Louis Catron's *Elements of Playwriting* has been a real labor of love. I've assigned this book to my introductory playwriting classes for over 15 years, and I've stuck with the book over that period of time because of the real values I believe it has for my students. In the process of updating it, I've read it more closely than ever before and have come to a new appreciation for the original author, his passion, his grasp of theatre, and his concern for the next generations of playwrights. What a privilege to be able to prepare an edition of the book that twenty-first-century playwrights will hopefully find useful and inspiring!

Those who have used the first edition of *Elements* will find quite a few changes in this version. I have intended to maintain the tone, spirit, and solid values of the original while bringing it fully into line with twenty-first-century theatre. Here are some of the changes that you may notice.

Quite a few plays that the original used as examples have fallen out of frequent usage in the past 25 years, and of course the 1993 original referenced no plays written after the end of the 1980s. While keeping examples from classics like *Tartuff*, various Shakespeare plays, *Glass Menagerie*, and *Death of a Salesman*, I have eliminated references to plays that have become unfamiliar to most students. I've also added examples from numerous plays written in the 1990s and since 2000. Of course, some of these will also eventually fade from usage, but I tried to select samples that have at least a fair chance of longevity.

Also within the text of the chapters, I have attempted to open the book up to a broader style of theatre that has become more and more established over the past 25 years. I have, for instance, removed most of the references to rules for playwriting, partly because I'm not sure we've had actual playwriting *rules* since the end of the neoclassical period and partly because I've noticed ever-increasing resistance to rule-oriented thinking amongst my students in the new millennium. In a similar mode,

I've eliminated most of the "shoulds," "musts," and other absolutes in the book's language. I've also included occasional examples of plays and dramaturgical practices that move away from the traditional, realistic, cause-and-effect approach that was fundamental to the first edition. These changes are the closest I've come to modifying the tone of the book. While some educators may find these changes disappointing, I believe that many more—and particularly our students who will write the plays of the twenty-first century—will find them helpful, liberating, and inspiring.

And, naturally, I've moved the book from the age of typewriters and exclusive hard-copy submissions via the postal service into that of Web-based research, word processors, and electronic submission processes.

In Chapter 10, I've changed the recommended format. The first edition utilized what the Dramatists Guild's *Resource Directory* calls "traditional format" with several tab settings across the page. I've instead recommended the more simplified mode the Guild calls "modern."

As far as overall structure, the biggest change is the addition of a new chapter, inserted after Chapter 7, which focuses on the playwright's responsibility to lay the groundwork for production elements. This chapter deals with such matters as casting, design elements, theatre architecture as it impacts audience/performer relationships, various staging modes, approaches to theatricality, and the uses and expectations of stage directions. Regarding the structure of the book, I also reversed the order of the chapters on plot and character, thus addressing plot before character. I did this simply because, in agreement with Aristotle, I consider plot to be of primary importance, and it made sense to me to deal with the shape of a play before focusing on the agents who carry out its action.

And finally, I've added a few additional reading resources at the end of most of the chapters that I hope will be useful to those who want to delve deeper into the book's subjects.

So raise a glass in appreciation of Louis Catron's vision, open this new edition of his book, dive in, and write on!

Norman A. Bert
Lubbock, Texas

Writers at Work
(Part One)

STAN: My head is tightening up. I'm all constricted inside. I just can't think. (*He thinks, then looks at EUGENE.*) This is hard, Gene. Really hard.

EUGENE: I know.

STAN: I won't give up if you don't give up.

EUGENE: I won't give up.

STAN: I love being a writer.

EUGENE: Me, too.

STAN: It's just the writing that's hard. . . . You know what I mean?

EUGENE: Yeah.

NEIL SIMON
Broadway Bound

1

Being a Playwright

> *I see the playwright as a lay preacher peddling the ideas of his time in popular form.*
>
> — AUGUST STRINDBERG
>
> *Never fear [the audience] nor despise it. Coax it, charm it, interest it, stimulate it, shock it now and then if you must, make it laugh, make it cry. but above all . . . never, never, never bore the living hell out of it.*
>
> — NÖEL COWARD

How do you become a playwright? What makes a *good* play? Where do you start? How does writing plays differ from writing essays, novels, or short stories? What techniques do professional writers recommend? What do you look for to revise your play? What do producers and directors look for in your play?

This book answers these and comparable questions. Here we examine what it means to "be a playwright." Later chapters discuss other aspects of the playwright's art and craft, constructing your play to suit theatre's special needs, shaping your ideas into theatrical form, bringing characters to life, composing effective dialogue, and writing stageworthy scripts.

Being a Playwright Means Appreciating Your Ancestry

When you become a playwright you join an elite group of civilization's most accomplished artists. Your oldest ancestor is the prehistoric shaman who used magic, costume, and pantomime-dance to enact scenes that enlightened tribal members trying to understand the mysteries of a confusing and sometimes hostile universe. Like that prophet of the past, you are a master storyteller who uses a special form of theatrical magic to communicate to audiences, giving them insight into a world that is no less confusing for being modern and illuminating mysteries that surround us.

You enter an arena made famous by playwrights who have been revered for their insightful, powerful tales of humans struggling not merely to survive but to endure. You join Sophocles, Aristophanes, Hrotsvitha, Molière, William Shakespeare, Aphra Behn, Henrik Ibsen, George Bernard Shaw, Lillian Hellman, Tennessee Williams, Arthur Miller, Neil Simon, Lorraine Hansberry, Samuel Beckett, Edward Albee, Harold Pinter, Tony Kushner, August Wilson, Martin McDonagh, Marsha Norman, Suzan-Lori Parks, and thousands of others whose plays shape public opinion, awake emotions, stimulate thought, and enlighten, amuse, and captivate millions.

You write for a unique art that over centuries has made major contributions to human growth and enjoyment. The theatre's accomplishments are remarkable, as Frank Whiting says in *An Introduction to the Theatre:*

> Without quibbling over which is the greatest of the arts, let us remember that the theatre makes its appeal on two levels: the aesthetic and the intellectual. On the aesthetic level the theatre, like music, painting, and dancing, makes its contribution to the emotional needs of man and to his hunger for the beautiful. On the intellectual level a tremendous proportion of the greatest ideas ever expressed by man have been expressed in dramatic form. Students of philosophy study Aeschylus, Goethe, Ibsen, and Shaw, as well as Plato, Schopenhauer, Nietzsche, and Dewey. No other branch of human learning can point with pride to a more impressive list of great names. No other field of literature can quite equal the drama in the total extent of its contributions.

Whiting's description of theatre's contributions is focused on playwrights—leaders in theatre's growth. Although his list of great playwrights is impressive, we can add more. For example, students of psychology study Sophocles and use his plays *Electra* and *Oedipus the King* to identify psychological dysfunctions such as the "Electra" and "Oedipal" complexes. Equally significant lists can be cited for theology, history, politics, sociology, biography, and other fields. Throughout history playwrights have been active in social protest and movements for reform in politics, society, medicine, economics, and the like.

One way to become aware of your ancestors' many contributions is to read their plays, selecting playwrights who have written about topics and characters that intrigue you. Solely reading a play, however, is not enough; you should see plays in production, carefully observing the writing techniques that make them come to life from page to stage.

Being a Playwright Starts with Knowing Who You Are

Membership in the distinguished community of playwrights starts with coming to grips with your personal beliefs, attitudes, and standards. These provide the foundation of your plays. You also examine your understanding of human behavior, discovering and taking note of the vast variety of human personalities and activities. These concepts lead you to create characters you'll believe in and care about. Those two steps give your plays special meaning and make them original works.

Many playwrights sense a strong need to communicate their deepest personal beliefs. A play that boils up from your inner self will be stronger because it expresses ideas important to you; the writing process will be easier and more enjoyable because you'll *want* to write, which will help motivate you to establish daily writing goals and maintain a writer's self-discipline. You want your plays to appeal to others—writing for the theatre is based on a desire to communicate—but that doesn't imply you diminish your own values by writing to please others. You first satisfy your own drive to communicate what you believe is important.

Theatrical excitement is a product of the playwright's passion and commitment. Think of your play as a personalized statement of your inner core: who you are, what you believe, what your vision of the world around you is. Write plays dealing with ideas and people that are most important to you. Substance comes with "I have an idea I *must* express through the stage," not "I'll write a play." The latter is an exercise, the former, a passion. Exercises are valuable learning tools to help you develop technique, but your goal is larger: You want to use the theatre to show your particular vision of your world. Personal involvement with your play's subject will be contagious, attracting producers, directors, actors, and audiences who will share your interest.

Identify Your Beliefs

Before you begin writing, identify what is most important to you, a process that for many playwrights is an insightful journey into self-discovery. Spend as much time as necessary writing your personal credo, a statement of your deepest convictions, beliefs, and standards. Although preparing your statement of "This I Believe" may take several weeks and result in dozens of pages, the investment of time and effort will net a rich return when you write your plays. Your credo becomes a treasure chest of precious jewels and gold that you use to create glittering characters and rich situations for effective plays.

Your written statement of convictions is deeply personal—there are no right or wrong beliefs—and focuses on topics that are highly important to you. For example, your credo may deal with such matters as family, love, or marriage; an individual's ambition, goals, and future; the significance of past experiences, loves, or hates; what it means to be selfish or giving; social problems such as AIDS, unwanted pregnancy and abortion, drugs, or the homeless; ethical dilemmas between right and wrong; and aspects of religion, relationship with a deity, or attitudes about false prophets.

Organize Your Beliefs by Priorities

When you've completed the first step of identifying your beliefs, it is time to put them in an order of priority, deciding which are most important to you. Once you've identified your ideas, you will be poised to consider playwriting's techniques, conventions, and standards, or producers, directors, and agents. Start your journey into being a playwright with a need to express a passion and write about a fire that ignites your inner being. From time to time revisit your credo and up-date it. You'll be surprised how you change over time, and you'll notice that writing plays has contributed significantly to learning about yourself.

Being a Playwright Means Studying People

Personal convictions, although highly important, are not enough for the playwright. Convictions, after all, can lead to essays, which *tell* the reader a point of view. You want to write plays that *show* those significant aspects of life. Being a playwright requires you to translate your abstract convictions into concrete, dimensional, interesting characters who investigate those beliefs through theatrical conflict, using actions and inactions, speeches and silences. Effective playwriting is based on the writer's fascination with human psychology, looking closely at people around you (including yourself, family, and friends) and the fictional characters who live in your imagination, awaiting your invitation to come to life in your plays.

Just as one major factor in becoming a playwright is identifying issues important to you, so an equally important part is recognizing the specific *human traits* you believe are most significant—characteristics you admire, respect, and love, as well as the qualities you dislike, reject, or despise. Awareness of these traits leads you to create dimensional characters in your play, and your beliefs about people help you create characters with qualities that are important to you, making you want, even need, to write.

Think about plays you have read or productions you have seen, and you'll find that you're remembering the characters. The Macbeths, Hamlets, Laura Wingfields, and Willy Lomans remain in audiences' memories because the playwrights' attitudes and beliefs about people created moving, interesting, memorable characters who often seem to have a real-life existence beyond the confines of the stage.

Become a Collector of Human Characters

Unlike many who soon forget most of the people they encounter, the playwright is likely to collect human personalities and characteristics. Collecting demands awareness. Pay close attention to the people you encounter daily. What seems to interest them, drive them? What are their obsessions? How do they express their values in words and behaviors, and in particular, do they have idiosyncratic ways of speaking or managing their bodies? How do they interact with others? How have their backgrounds and their occupations shaped them? What are their fears, their hopes? What occupies their minds? How do they make decisions? Of course, you can't analyze every person you meet, but you can certainly note behaviors and characteristics that stand out. Consider making it a practice, at the end of each day, to jot down one or two things about people that you observed that day. You'll find that your awareness of people will develop and that your observations will enliven the characters you create.

The man who writes about himself and his own time is the only man who writes about all people and about all time.

— George Bernard Shaw

Being a Playwright Involves a Sense of Construction; Being a Playwright Involves a Sense of Discovery

On the one hand, writing plays is like designing and building bridges. Like the bridge builder, you are involved in planning, designing, crafting, and constructing—in a very real sense plays are *built*—and you focus on frame, shape, and style. Both playwright and bridge builder are visionaries, imagining a connection where none exists; both seek to take people where they've never been. You face practical and aesthetic considerations as you design a construction that will take the traveler to the specific destination you've planned. Just as engineering principles guide the construction of a bridge that will not collapse, so there are fundamental concepts involved in writing a play that will hold the stage. Because of this relationship between constructing and playwriting, the writer of a play is called a *playwright*—one who constructs a play in the same way that one who builds a ship is called a *shipwright*.

On the other hand, the playwright is also an adventurer who enters uncharted territories. Like an explorer, you may enter *terra incognita* with a variety of tools and skills and a sense of where you may be going, what you may find there, and how it may change you and the people who follow you. But you don't know everything about your route or what you will encounter as you step across that river into that unknown land that will be your play. To change the metaphor, you are like a gardener who plants a seed and watches it grow. Hopefully you've selected good seed, and you've placed it in the appropriate soil with the right exposure to the sun. You have a sense of how much water and fertilizer to give it. But you don't know exactly what shape it will take or how much fruit it will produce. And you watch with amazement as the young plant seems to have a life of its own while it grows to maturity.

Some playwrights approach their tasks like engineers building a bridge; others approach a new play like an explorer of a new land or a gardener planting a seed. Whether engineer or explorer, both need tools, knowledge and skills, and an understanding of processes and principles. Without these necessities, the bridge will collapse, the expedition will fail, and the plant will die. This book is intended to give you the beginnings of what you need to build your play, to map that new territory, to grow a lush, productive garden.

Being a Playwright Means Writing
Stageworthy Plays, Not "Closet Dramas"

You write plays that need theatre's magical alchemy to make their full impact. Directors look for stageworthy qualities in your play and reject it if they are absent. Although "stageworthy" is admittedly difficult to define because tastes, styles, and imaginations vary, here we introduce some of the basic qualities of a stageworthy play, and later chapters will examine the concept in more detail. You will develop personal ideas about stageworthiness as you continue studying the art of playwriting. We can start our definition by examining negative examples, plays that aren't stageworthy, often called "closet dramas."

What Is "Closet Drama"?

You may read some literary works that look like plays—they appear to be dialogues between individuals—but you sense they simply wouldn't work on stage. We call them closet dramas, an author's mental or stylistic exercise, more debates or excursions in language than dramatic action, and the opposite of a play meant for the stage. "Closet" in this sense refers to a small drawing room where literary people congregate. These nonplays are valuable negative examples that help you distinguish what is stageworthy.

Examples of closet dramas start with Plato, the Greek philosopher who wrote "Dialogues," apparently designed to be spoken but actually are intellectual philosophical exercises best read privately. In his "Dialogues" you find individuals (one hesitates to call them characters) who have no emotional involvement or contact with the issues, and the dialogues are abstract debates without evolving and building action. The

Roman playwright Seneca wrote "plays" such as *Octavia*, exercises that transform poorly to the stage because they use stereotypical heroines and heroes who only slightly resemble humans. They, too, debate each other without feeling, personal involvement, or concern about the outcome. Closet drama was especially popular during the Victorian age when poets wrote "dramas" that were stylistic exercises without dramatic action, perhaps best exemplified by Swinburne's *Chastelard* and *Mary Stuart*. Whatever the literary or intellectual merits of such closet dramas, they simply are not theatrical.

What Is a "Stageworthy" Play?

Unlike a closet drama, a play fulfills its author's purpose when it is staged, a process demanding active contributions from actors, director, designers, and audience. Such a play passionately expresses the playwright's vision; conflict sparks plausible and compelling action; credible and dimensional characters have a life of their own; dialogue is easily speakable by actors and instantly understandable by audiences; events are compressed economically to achieve intensity; and the combined effects flow from beginning to end. All achieve maximum impact when given life onstage.

Throughout this book we'll cite examples of stageworthy plays, noting that each must be staged for full effect because reading it silently to oneself in the privacy of one's home will not fully realize the work. We'll discuss how you write works for the live theatre using theme, conflict, action, language, voices of the performers, visual aspects of action, and characters' emotional involvement. The goal is to help you learn appropriate techniques so you can create equally stageworthy plays.

Being a Playwright Means Understanding, Using, Modifying, and Challenging Accepted Principles and Guidelines of Drama

The idea of rules for playwrights or any other creative artist is controversial. Some teachers urge new writers to "learn the rules before you break them." While this advice may be sound, playwrights who are acquainted with the history of drama may well ask, "Which rules?"— because the principles of dramaturgy have been in constant flux ever since Aeschylus.

Usually, those who advocate following the rules are referring to what might be called *traditional dramaturgy.* This understanding of drama was first described by the Greek philosopher Aristotle in his important work, *The Poetics.* Aristotle understood the world to be a logical, balanced cosmos in which human beings were expected to act in accord with *dike* (justice); the principles of drama that he taught reflected this worldview. His ideas were hardened into rules by the neoclassicists in the seventeenth and eighteenth centuries. In the early nineteenth century, Eugene Scribe and others who were interested in exploiting new audiences adapted these rules into the principles of *the well-made play*. This approach to writing plays lives on today in popular drama including a modified form of American cinema.

But, oh, the challenges to traditional dramaturgy! While Scribe was entertaining middle-class audiences, the Romantics—bursting onto the scene and rejecting neoclassicism—insisted that art is the product of genius, not rules. They called for dramas and novels that laid aside conventions, expressed powerful emotions, and depicted human beings as bound for the stars but cursed by their physical limitations. And then, responding to the birth of sociology and the discoveries of Charles Darwin, the realists and naturalists, near the end of the nineteenth century, rejected the manipulations and happy endings of the well-made play and insisted that plays depict believable human beings living their lives conditioned by heredity and environment.

But even while realism was on the grow, expressionists, rebelling against scientism and the technology that they sensed was threatening the human spirit, rejected cause-and-effect structures and wrote wildly distorted plays with antiheros and exotic scenery. Then Bertolt Brecht and American writers like Clifford Odets, witnessing the apparent failure of capitalism in the Great Depression, combined expressionist structures with elements borrowed from Asian theatre and created a didactic form Brecht called *epic theatre*. Soon, having experienced the seeming failure of Western civilization in two world wars, writers like Samuel Beckett and Eugène Ionesco created yet another nonrealistic drama called *absurdism*, which put existentialist principles on stage. As the twentieth century grew to a close and the twenty-first century dawned, artists of all sorts rejected modernism with its confidence in progress, the future, and Western standards of quality. They turned to the past, to non-Western traditions, to the experiences and viewpoints of women, gays and lesbians, African Americans, Latino/as, and other minorities and created a plethora of forms roughly grouped together as *postmodernism*. And again, theatre and drama developed new approaches that utilized some aspects of traditional dramaturgy while rejecting or reinterpreting other aspects.

What are new playwrights to make of this history? What "rules" are they to learn and follow? In the first place, serious playwrights have a deep interest in dramatic structures—the shape of plots, the kinds of characters that carry out the plots, the nature of the dialogue the characters speak, the visual and aural elements that share the characters and their actions with the audience. As a new playwright, commit yourself to learning everything you can about these structures. Secondly, notice that none of the movements mentioned above embraced change for the mere sake of being original; instead, they were driven and inspired by their understanding of the world and the needs of society around them. As a new playwright, give attention to your credo and drink deep of the world around you. Ask yourself what playwriting structures match what you believe and observe. Third, immerse yourself in drama past and present. Read as many plays as you can from the Greeks down to the most recent off-Broadway innovations. And attend the theatre whenever and wherever you can. The more you read and the more you experience, the more you will learn about the possibilities of your art

No one knows what the future holds for drama and playwriting. History, however, demonstrates that traditional dramaturgy in its various forms has survived for two and a half millennia. Its longevity is due, at least in part, to its basis in storytelling; everyone has always enjoyed a good story well told. Traditional dramaturgy provides a good starting place for learning the playwright's craft. For that reason, much of this book will focus on lessons learned from Aristotle, the well-made play, and realism. Pay attention to these approaches to drama. And then, as you find them unsuitable for expressing your perceptions of your world, modify, break, or replace them with approaches that work in your life, in your world, and on your stages.

THEATRICAL DIRECTORS DESCRIBE
WHAT THEY LOOK FOR IN PLAYS

As a director, deciding on whether to direct a play, I ask the following questions: Am I engaged by the play? Do I care about what the playwright cares about? Is his way of revealing what we both care about unique? Is his voice a valid one? Is the structure of the play essentially dramatic? Is the spine of the play—a complete story with revelation and conclusion—embedded in the material somehow?

— LLOYD RICHARDS

[When I am deciding whether to direct a play] I look to see if the play is relevant in some particular way to life as the artist has experienced it.

— MARSHALL W. MASON

The single quality that jumps out of every script I like is honesty. The kind of text that attracts me is one that comes right from the writer's gut. . . . I respond to writing that comes from the heart and isn't essentially literary.

— ARVIN BROWN

Being a Playwright Means
Writing, Writing, and Writing

Writing is a difficult art to master, requiring devotion, study, and practice if one is to succeed. Of the various forms of writing, playwriting presents particular problems, according to well-known authors who have written both novels and plays, such as Thornton Wilder (whose novels and plays include, respectively, *The Bridge of San Luis Rey* and *Our Town*, both winners of Pulitzer Prizes) and James Kirkwood (known as a novelist for *Good Times/Bad Times*, as a playwright for *P.S. Your Cat Is Dead!*, and as one of the writers of *A Chorus Line*, for which he shared a Pulitzer Prize). Such writers say they find plays more difficult to write—as Wilder says, drama "is far harder than the novel"—and it follows that it requires of you even more devoted study, practice, and perseverance.

Write to Learn to Write

An essential step toward mastering the art and craft of playwriting is convincing yourself that above all else you *must* write. If you want to be a playwright, write. If you want to learn how to marry structure with content, write. If you want to find ideas, awaken your imagination, turn on your vision, sharpen your eye for people's hearts and your insight into their problems and struggles, understand yourself more clearly and sympathetically, and come to grips with what's most important to you in your corner of the world, you must write.

The Blank Page

The empty computer screen or blank sheet of paper challenges the writer like an antagonist. On its side are all the old enemies, such as procrastination, hypercritical attitudes about your writing, self-induced doubts about the value of your basic idea, a hunger to achieve perfection but a paralyzing fear that you won't reach your goal, and avoidance temptations that lead you to do *anything*—sharpen pencils, get coffee, clean closets, watch television, text your friends, wash the dog, wax the car—rather than write. One writer wryly says her friends and relatives can tell when she's having trouble with her play because that's when her correspondence to them sharply increases.

You're not alone when you have difficulties getting started: Every writer fights to overcome self-defeatist attitudes. Believe you will win. On your side is your hunger to express yourself, your love of writing and theatre, your dedication to your goal, your pride in accomplishment, your sense of self-worth, dogged determination to prove to yourself you can succeed, and the knowledge that even the largest project gets done one page at a time.

In reality, that blank page isn't your enemy; it's your opportunity. That empty space begs for your ideas, your vision, and your passion.

Engage it. Make it your friend. Determine that right now you'll fill at least one page with parts of a play. Write that first line; it need not be great, but it needs to be written. When that first page is full, do another. Soon you'll have completed 4 pages. Write 4 pages a day for a month, and you'll finish 120 pages, the size of a full-length play.

Keep your expectations reasonable. Seek perfection, of course, but not all at once, and definitely not on the first draft. Get your play written, going from beginning to end. Avoid qualitative judgments while you're writing. Only after you've completed a first draft should you start demanding higher quality of your play and yourself, depending on the revision process (see Chapter 8) to improve your script.

It Must Come to Writing *Today*

> "The rule is, jam tomorrow, and jam yesterday—but never jam *today*."
>
> "It must come sometimes to 'jam today,'" Alice objected.
>
> "No, it can't," said the Queen. "It's jam every *other* day. Today isn't any *other* day, you know."

According to the Queen's wonderfully wacky Wonderland logic, Alice would never get any jam, and if the Queen's rules dictate a writer's life, he or she would never get anything written. As a playwright, convince yourself that if you want to write, it must come to writing *today*, not that other day that never comes.

Identify the best time of day for you to write. Every writer's biorhythms are unique, so find the time that fits you best. Then make a date with yourself to write regularly—every day, every other day, every Saturday and Sunday, whatever. Schedule a reasonable time to devote to each session—an hour, two hours, whatever works for you. You'll often find that once you get going, the process feeds on itself and you can be truly productive. And never stop at a good stopping place like the end of a scene. If you do, you'll have to begin from a dead start the next session. Instead, stop in the middle of a scene, even the middle of a sentence, when you know exactly what comes next. In the next session, you'll find that you can pick up the thread immediately, and *voila!* you're on your way.

The Serendipity Factor

Determine to write regularly, even if that means sitting at the keyboard and typing dialogue that has no connection with a known play. The point of this effort is partly to learn to think of writing as an active, not a passive, searching process, and partly to encourage what can be called the "serendipity factor" or the ability to make desirable discoveries by apparent accident. The act of writing can help you make those fortunate discoveries that stimulate a flow of ideas for more writing.

You can test the validity of the serendipity factor with a simple experiment: Invent two characters, give them specific names, and make them begin talking about anything. Write as quickly as you can. The initial dialogue may appear pointless, but after a dozen pages the characters take on life and dimension and you'll begin to think of ways to place the characters in a more meaningful situation.

Such exercises show that the only way to write is simply to write and that nothing gets written while you wait for a flash of divine inspiration. On the other hand, creative ideas will come if you make a situation that encourages them. As has been frequently observed, "Writing is nine-tenths perspiration and one-tenth inspiration." Convince yourself that only writing produces good writing.

PLAYWRIGHTS DESCRIBE THEIR WORK HABITS

I find it almost impossible to write anytime but in the morning, when I have more energy to write. . . . I am a compulsive writer. I have tried to stop working and I am bored to death. . . . It takes a physical toll of your nervous energies. You've got to do all kinds of things to try to make yourself stand up under it.

— TENNESSEE WILLIAMS

I write the first draft in longhand in an exercise book. I type the second— making changes in the process—and then go over it with a pen before retyping it again. There may be any number of drafts before I'm satisfied.

— ARNOLD WESKER

I'm usually up around six, and I'm almost always at the typewriter by eight and I write until twelve or one. Usually.

— WILLIAM INGE

Special Advantages of Being a Playwright

You'll find that being a playwright brings both challenges and advantages. The challenges often appear overwhelming. There'll be times you aren't sure you'll win the battle of marrying form, structure, characterization, and dialogue to express your vision. On the other hand, one major advantage is the feeling of accomplishment when you create a work of art. Each victory will sustain you through future struggles.

The Excitement of Playwriting

Theatre's impact on others.   Through theatre you have a remarkable opportunity to influence audiences. Many examples could be cited, but perhaps one of the more striking is described by playwright Arthur Miller in *Timebends: A Life.*

> As sometimes happened later on during the run, there was no applause at the final curtain of the first performance [of *Death of a Salesman*]. Strange things began to go on in the audience. With the curtain down, some people stood to put their coats on and then sat again, some, especially men, were bent forward covering their faces, and others were openly weeping. People crossed the theatre to stand quietly talking with one another. It seemed forever before someone remembered to applaud, and then there was no end to it. I was standing at the back and saw a distinguished-looking elderly man being led up the aisle; he was talking excitedly into the ear of what seemed to be his male secretary or assistant. This, I learned, was Bernard Gimbel, head of the department store chain, who that night gave an order that no one in his stores was to be fired for being overage.

Being a playwright is a deeply satisfying way to communicate your ideas to others, as Miller did, perhaps changing their perception of their actions. Writing plays can be—must be—a personally enriching experience. It also can be remarkably educational: Writing plays, especially creating characters, will give you increased sensitivity and insight into others, and into yourself.

EXERCISES

Each chapter concludes with exercises that will help you develop your art and craft. Always *write* your responses—you are, after all, a writer—and give yourself ample time to do each exercise thoroughly.

Record answers to these and other exercises in your personal *Playwright's Journal*, a large, three-ring notebook with a number of tab dividers for various categories such as "Play in Progress," "Next Play," "Daily Journal," "Calendar and Writing Schedule," "Dialogue," "Situations," "Diary of Writing," "Ideas for Plays," "Newspaper and Magazine Clippings," "Inspirational Quotations," "Exercises," and the like.

1. What are the strongest inner beliefs that control your being? What most awakens your interest? First list your beliefs, the topics that you care about more than any others, and then write about your feelings for each. Think of your statements as deeply personal expressions; no one will evaluate your answers, and there is no right or wrong response except that you should express your own sense of truth. Write several pages about each passion. Your detailed statements will become materials for plays you'll write.

2. What human traits do you value because you think they are praiseworthy? List them. What actions show those values? Give illustrations.

3. What personality traits strike you as negative? List them. Describe actions that show those qualities.

4. Make a list of stageworthy plays you've seen in production. Although it is difficult to isolate the playscript from the production, try to focus on the play itself, not actors, directors, or designers.

5. Using that list, describe why those plays held the stage. What made them work? What qualities appear essential for a play to work onstage? How did those plays grasp audience attention? Did you perceive a playwright's passion? What in the play's action attracted you? What aspects of characterization were most interesting? How does dialogue contribute to making a play stageworthy?

6. Schedule your writing time. At what hours will you write? For how long? How many days a week? Construct a calendar that assigns you specific writing periods.

7. Decide how you'll measure your writing period. Will you write a specific number of hours? Or will you write until you've completed a minimum number of pages? Write your assignment on your calendar.

Each morning my characters
greet me with misty faces
willing, though chilled, to muster
for another day's progress
through the dazzling quicksand
the marsh of blank paper.

— John Updike

How can you write if you can't cry?

— Ring Lardner

ADDITIONAL READING ON THE TOPICS OF THIS CHAPTER

Catron, Louis E. *Playwriting: Writing, Producing, and Selling Your Play.* 2nd ed. Waveland, 1990. Ch. 4 "The Credo." More details on this important part of the playwright's life.

Neipris, Janet. *To Be a Playwright*. Routledge, 2005. Ch. 1 "The Twelve Habits of Successful Playwrights." Wisdom from the head of a leading dramatic writing program.

Smiley, Sam with Norman A. Bert. *Playwriting: The Structure of Action*. 2nd ed. Yale University Press, 2005. Ch. 1 "Vision" and ch. 11 "A Way of Life." An in-depth look at what it means to be a playwright.

2

What Makes a Play?

The fantastic thing about the theatre is that it can make something be seen that's invisible, and that's where my interest in theatre is—that you can be watching this thing happening with actors and costumes and light and set and language, and even plot, and something emerges from beyond that, and that's the image part that I'm looking for, that sort of added dimension.

— SAM SHEPARD

Being a playwright requires a sensitivity to the special demands of theatre, finding answers to the question, "What makes a play?" For theatrical writing *construction* is important because in a real sense plays are built as much as written. Continued experience writing plays, plus reading and seeing other playwrights' works, will help you establish personal concepts of what makes a play, especially what creates a good play.

This chapter focuses on the elements that make a play, helping you transform your ideas from rough form into a theatrical work. In particular we look at basic concepts of stageworthy plays, helping you write plays that will interest producers, directors, and actors, and that will excite and satisfy audiences, thus giving you a better chance of being produced. Since no single definition of a play can satisfy all playwrights, here are two sample definitions to consider.

A play deals with materials that "simply cannot be expressed by any other means," according to Eugène Ionesco, and it is constructed with "a complexity of words, movements, gestures that convey a vision of the world inexpressible in any other way." As Sam Shepard says, theatre transforms the invisible into the visible. It can be—many argue it must be—more magical than any other form of writing.

Two Definitions of "a Play"

First, a traditional definition: A play is a structured and unified story, comic or dramatic, complete in itself with a beginning, middle, and end, that expresses the playwright's passion and vision of life, shows unfolding conflict that builds to a climax, and deals with dimensional lifelike humans who have strong emotions, needs, and objectives that motivate them to take action. It is constructed with a plausible and probable series of events, written to be performed and therefore told with speeches and actions plus silences and inactions, projected by actors from a stage to an audience that is made to believe the events are happening as they watch.

And then a broader definition: A play is an event that creates or recreates human experience. It is enacted for and in the presence of its audience by live performers utilizing visual and aural elements including human activities. It is done to engage the audience by intensifying their awareness and understanding of life. A play *script* is a written plan for staging a play.

A Play Is Not a Novel

In some respects you are like the novelist, poet, essayist, newspaper reporter, screenwriter, or even sermon writer. You share with them passion and a commitment to writing, a special delight in words and ideas, the need to express a personal vision, fascination with the mysteries of human behavior, misgivings about social or political trends, dedication to self-improvement, the ability to work long solitary hours, a hunger for perfection, self-discipline that focuses your time and energy on your projects, and an undefinable joy when you see your work in print or, in your case, onstage. You are driven by a compulsion to use your art to make connections between what others know and see, and an ineffable unknown that only you envision.

A Play Is a Blueprint for Actors and Directors

More enlightening than similarities, however, are the differences between playwriting and all other forms of writing. Unlike the novelist, whose final product is a set form that is captured forever within the covers of a book, your play is interpreted and extended by talented directors, designers, and actors who dedicate their skills to bringing your play to life. With each new production your play is reborn, surprisingly different because of theatrical creativity and interpretation. In this sense your script is a blueprint designed for theatre personnel, and you write a stage-worthy play by remaining keenly aware of their needs and their methods of communicating your play to an audience.

A Play Speaks to a Group Consciousness

Novelists write for one reader at a time; you write for a group con-sciousness. The novel's reader, if confused, can back up pages or even chapters to reread illuminating passages; your play must maintain an instant clarity so the audience member will have no questions about cru-cial facts. Novelists expect that a reader will put down the book for a period of time; you must grasp the audience's full, uninterrupted atten-tion during the entire play.

Think of performances you've seen that captivated audiences throughout. What were the factors that caused the audience to concen-trate on the play? As you remember such plays, quite likely you will recall the projection of strong emotions, conflicts between intriguing char-acters who were deeply involved in the action, the examination of signifi-cant issues, suspense and concern for the outcome, and crisp dialogue.

Plays Communicate with Dialogue and Action

A novelist or short story writer often uses expository passages to describe the environment, events, scenery, characters, characters' thoughts and feelings, and the like. Playwrights usually do not. You focus on what characters say and refuse to say, plus actions they do and do not take—all communications to the audience. Novelists or sermon writers can directly state moral points or lessons, but playwrights communicate such information indirectly, using dialogue and actions.

Shakespeare's *Macbeth*, for example, has powerful actions that convey the play's thematic core about the destructiveness of a quest for absolute power. Imagine a novelist's version of the same story—expository pas-sages describing Macbeth's inner hungers and struggles, his environ-ment, choices, and, ultimately, the reasons for his downfall. In contrast, imagine a stage production with Macbeth showing his tension and con-flict, the sounds of the language, the sweep of color and movement, and a sense of seeing action happening now.

Plays Are Set in the Present, Moving to a Future

Present tense. Characters in a novel *did* or *said* this or that; in a play the characters *are doing* actions and *are speaking* dialogue *now*. The distinction is vital. A novel is written in the past tense, relating events that took place and were completed before the reader picked up the book; your play lives in a perpetual present tense, depicting events that are unfolding this very moment in front of the audience.

Future tense.   If the present tense distinguishes a play from a novel, a sense of impending future distinguishes a play with dramatic impact from a nondramatic script. Your play's characters and actions have a lively, ever-present sense of future. The current actions of a play's characters constantly move toward some impending goal; plays have forward-looking action; present actions convey potential consequences.

Present and future tenses create requirements for a playwright. If you find that your characters continually refer to past events, ask yourself if you should reset your play in that past situation. Equally, if your characters seem to lack interest in the future, ask if you should recreate them to have specific goals that are highly important to them. As we discuss in later chapters, sensitivity to your characters' present and future will greatly ease problems when constructing plot and motivating characters.

Plays' Movement in Time and Place

Novels, like screenplays, are enhanced by frequent and sweeping movements through time and space. Plays, on the other hand, tend to be more powerful when tightly focused. Novels often seek to depict a large number of scenes to show the story's large universe; plays compress action into one whole that represents that larger universe. One appeal of a novel is its ability to view life through a wide-angle, even panoramic, lens. Your play, however, gains strength with a narrower focus on specific actions that are most significant to your vision.

Plays Show Rather than Tell

A play must show what characters are thinking and feeling; a novel may *tell* and describe. A novelist may editorialize explicitly about concepts regarding life or the novel's meaning; you communicate the same concepts primarily through actions, not direct statements. A novelist can describe what characters are thinking; you show what characters are thinking by their actions and inactions, speeches and silences. You work on the time-honored premise that "actions speak louder than words" to show the play's thought and the characters' goals and emotions.

The Play's Objective and Collective Point of View

Fiction writers may choose to write from a character's viewpoint, how that character sees events. They may, for example, use an omniscient point of view to relate any character's perception, a first-person view that uses the word *I* to take the reader into the mind of the major character, or a third-person viewpoint that does not use the word *I* but otherwise focuses on what one character feels, believes, hears, and sees.

Playwrights, in contrast, write with an objective and collective point of view. You represent all characters—one way of writing plays is to "become" each character while he or she is speaking and reacting—and you seek to show each character's individual attitudes, emotions, goals, hopes, and dreams.

Plays Are Written for Actors to Communicate to the Audience's Eye and Ear

A stageworthy play is written for actors to speak and do. The novelist expects readers will enjoy perfectly constructed and balanced sentences, reread favorite passages, look up unfamiliar words, or check a literary concordance to find sources of allusions to poems or other forms of literature. In contrast, your audiences respond to the overall action and characterization in movement, not to individual literary moments. Passages that call attention to themselves in a play are considered distracting and therefore are seldom acceptable. Audiences must be able to understand words and references immediately, requiring you to craft dialogue that makes things clear by context.

A Play Faces Added Revisions

Although editors may require some rewriting, novelists, short story authors, and other writers are finished when their projects are accepted by a publisher. In contrast, the playwright faces more revisions, seeking clarity, structural strength, action, depth of characterization, and lively dialogue. Many such aspects of your play are tested by the crucible of performance, and a play that looks correct on paper may turn out to need major or minor changes when theatre personnel begin bringing it to life. Once a producer or director accepts your script, you should expect to continue making major revisions during rehearsals while the play is being put on its feet, and yet again after judging audience reaction to your play in performance.

Plays Require Conflict

Novels may succeed without conflict, but plays rarely do. Conflict is so essential for effective plays that a "law of conflict" has become an expected part of successful theatrical writing. Conflict fuels the motor that propels your play forward. Without conflict your play is likely to lack movement, issues, questions raised and examined, character changes in response to stimuli, and suspense to hold audience attention. Conflict creates the dramatic tension necessary for plays, comic or tragic. A play without conflict is very likely to be a play without dramatic impact.

Conflict Is Force against Force

Conflict most typically is one individual (protagonist) seeking a goal (objective) but opposed by comparable forces (one or more antagonists). For example, conflict is boy (protagonist) highly motivated to want girl (objective) but confronted with parents (antagonists) who violently oppose the match. This particular model has had countless successful retellings in theatre literature, perhaps most notably in *Romeo and Juliet* and *West Side Story*. But the model isn't restricted to boy-wants-girl or even love: Variations of that basic structure occur in countless other successful plays that deal with quite different plots, themes, and characters but nonetheless are built with a protagonist seeking a goal and facing strong opposition. The result is conflict.

Think of the basic protagonist-goal versus antagonist-opposition outline as a skeleton that you can use to create numerous other dramatic conflicts. To that framework you add flesh, intellect, emotion, and meaning by investing your unique vision, beliefs, and voice, turning the framework into your own original statement.

Opposing Forces Need Equal Strengths

If a play's action is to be sustained, opposing forces need to be equal. The zeal of the parental objections must match the boy's fervor for the girl, and the balance of power continually shifts, as in a prizefight, during the course of the play. First one force appears to win, then the other. One force may doubt the wisdom of the action, creating internal conflict; another force may call in outside reinforcements. There are reversals and discoveries; obstacles are encountered, destroyed, and reborn. The intensity of the struggle grows as each side senses victory. These shifts in balance create suspense, compelling the audience to concentrate on your play.

Conflict Expresses the Play's Meaning

How do you communicate the play's overall intellectual meaning if you can't use didactic speeches that state the questions, solution, and concept? Through action. What the characters do indicates the play's core questions and the playwright's vision of answers to dilemmas.

Playwrights often tackle ethical issues, changing abstract questions into concrete human situations. Many illustrations could be cited, but we mention only a few here:

- We must keep clear the distinction between justice and revenge: *Medea* by Euripides.

- One should value people more highly than money: *The Miser* by Molière.

- A woman must have the right to be respected as a person: *A Doll's House* by Henrik Ibsen.

• The world is on the cusp of huge social and political changes: *Angels in America, Part I* by Tony Kushner.

In all such plays, the moral lesson is not verbalized but is shown through conflict.

Conflict and Abstract Forces

Conflict can involve the individual against abstract forces, such as self or society, but because drama requires showing instead of telling, such conflict becomes most effective when that abstraction is made concrete by one or more specific characters in the play. For example, on one level *Hamlet* involves internal conflict, Hamlet against himself, but that is shown through the external conflicts between Hamlet and Claudius and Gertrude. Those external conflicts illuminate the internal struggles Hamlet experiences.

Conflict Creates Dimensional Characters

Conflict enhances characterization because struggles show characters making mental and emotional changes; without struggles, characters would remain the same. Each twist and turn of the conflict forces characters to find new ways to deal with new situations, thus showing new dimensional qualities. Characters would lack motivation to change without those variations that result from conflict's struggles. As the balance of power shifts, characters necessarily must respond to stimuli and, therefore, change. Struggle makes characters become more dimensional and interesting.

Conflict Provides the Structure of a Play

Plot is more easily understood when you think of it as the structure of conflict. Drama is the art of the showdown, conflict in action, the play's characters at work in the present to achieve a goal in the future while attempting to overcome conflicts such as obstacles, reversals, and complications. *Hamlet* contains a number of showdown scenes, such as between Hamlet and the Ghost, Hamlet and Gertrude, Hamlet and his uncle, and Hamlet and Laertes.

In plays like *Oedipus the King*, *Hamlet*, and *A Doll's House*, the sequential order of conflict makes up the structure of plot. A given play's plot begins with an initial conflict, which sparks the protagonist into the action that will drive the plot; the middle contains the building struggles that develop the plot; and the end resolves that conflict. Conflict is a major tool that the playwright tool uses to build a plot and tell a story.

Conflict draws the audience into the play, involving them in the action. Many people avoid conflicts in their own lives, but almost everyone enjoys watching conflict; otherwise the spectator seats in sports arenas would be empty, not full of wildly cheering fans. And conflict provides a sense of momentous events in progress in contrast to a sense that "nothing happens." Characters in conflict fascinate audiences. Audiences empathize with the characters' struggles to overcome crises, problems, emergencies, and complications.

Selectivity: Drama Is an Interpretation of Life, Not Real Life

Imagine a large party, a familiar real-life situation. Everybody's talking at once, music is blaring, and people are milling about. In the middle of the chaos, two people are having a violent argument. Others watch or perhaps leave. Some get drunk and begin to sing. Imagine the playwright tape-records the party. Will the event, transcribed word for word, make a play?

Or imagine two people arriving at a restaurant. They are led to a table. They sit. They chat. Someone takes their order. They continue to chat while they wait for dinner. Drinks arrive. They chat. They wait. Dinner arrives. They chat while they eat. Again, this is real life, but will it make a play?

In both instances the answer is, "Not likely." The playwright interested in dramatizing those scenes would have to make choices, a process of selectivity that is a vital part of art. The playwright would seek a way to represent those aspects that appear most important and that can be shaped into dramatic action.

Plays are based on life and show your vision of reality, but they are never real life. Instead, plays are artistic representations of the playwright's perception of certain aspects of life. You *select* from life. This distinction can help you understand the need to shape materials in a way that permits dramatization.

If you want to write about the party, for example, you will select the most important events and shape the action to make it dramatic. You might decide to place the party offstage to permit focus on the arguing couple. Alternatively, you might start the play an hour or so after the party, assume the couple has just arrived home, and dramatize the couple's argument.

Plays Are Complete in Themselves

A play is a holistic communication, complete in itself and containing all necessary information. It cannot depend on clarification from external sources such as announcements or notes in programs given to audiences, author's explanations, or audience knowledge of other plays, novels, or contemporary or historical events. Explanatory footnotes and stage directions, while certainly useful to production personnel, are communicated to audiences only through the dialogue and actions of the performance.

Plays Have a Beginning, Middle, and End

A play is likely to have a beginning, middle, and end. Although this observation appears elementary, adherence to it can help solve most structural problems. You may have seen plays that jumped into action so quickly, you felt confused by the lack of an orientation to the characters or situation; and you've probably seen plays that seemed to stop rather than end. Such plays illustrate the importance of effective beginnings and endings. You may also have seen plays that begin examining a major question, then suddenly wrap up the pieces and end too quickly, without probing the question in sufficient detail. Such plays illustrate the need for a sustained middle.

An effective beginning, middle, and end will be artistically balanced, admittedly a rather vague and subjective standard. That requirement defies exact specification because you are writing a play, not following a recipe for a soufflé. The point is that you give each portion its due. It can help to think of these three parts as the protagonist's movements. At the beginning he or she starts a major action, motivated to achieve a goal. During the middle the protagonist struggles to achieve that purpose. At the end he or she succeeds or fails, and in the process that character, and likely one or more other characters, gain new insights, which the audience also perceives.

The content and structure of the play will dictate how much importance is placed on each of these three elements. No one can insist that the beginning must be fifteen percent of the whole, the middle has to be seventy percent, and the ending will be fifteen percent, but those percentages might at least suggest the relative importance of each part of the triad. Note that the middle dominates because it contains action, movements of the plot, and development of the characters, and it occupies most of the time of the play.

Of course there are plays like Danai Gurira's *Eclipsed* and Lucas Hnath's *The Christians* that end with basic questions unanswered, but think carefully before you decide to take this route. How a play ends has a great deal to do with its basic meaning and its impact, so make sure your ending clearly expresses what you want to communicate to the audience.

Avoid Cinematic Writing

One of the litmus tests of a good play is that it is not a television script in disguise. I think, "Could this only work in the theater? Could this be better done as a movie with close-ups and angles, or not?" I think theater should stick with what it and nothing else can provide: language, imagination, dream.

— Eric Overmyer

Many theatrical directors are distressed by plays characterized by loose cinematic writing, with style and technique more appropriate for television or motion pictures than for the theatre. Such scripts typically have numerous brief scenes, often with no beginning, middle, or end, and many episodic jumps in time and space. Avoiding cinematic writing improves your chances for production of your play. But, since most playwrights have seen more movies and TV dramas or sitcoms than they have seen or read plays, they can easily slip into cinematic writing without even realizing it.

Danger Signals of Cinematic Writing

Learn to recognize certain danger flags signaling cinematic thinking that may permeate your play. For example, you're thinking of a camera's dolly movement if your play starts with the characters, say, walking through a mall, entering a shop to browse, and picking up small items the audience must see. You're thinking of a camera's zoom lens if the audience is to see a small prop, such as the contents of a letter, or if the audience is to recognize a character's emotions by "a glint in her eye." More dangerous, because corrective revision can be difficult, you're thinking of cinematic storytelling techniques if your play makes frequent jumps in time and space or demands large-scale physical activity like car chases.

Movies and television tell stories more with visual qualities and less with dialogue, the opposite of stage writing. Screenwriters talk about "opening up" a story by including more characters and scenes, as illustrated by movie adaptations of plays; playwrights intensify the story by focusing on fewer characters and only the most essential locales. Movies are at their best with large, sweeping physical action, illustrated by motion pictures such as *Alien* and *Raiders of the Lost Ark*. Plays are at their best when focused on psychological action, such as *A Streetcar Named Desire*, *Who's Afraid of Virginia Woolf?* and Amy Herzog's *Belleville*.

Dramatic Action Must Be
Possible, Plausible, and Probable

A play must be true to its own logic, which starts by establishing its ground rules or universe in the opening action. That logic cannot be violated later. A play can deal successfully with imaginative fantasy, science fiction projections into the future, or other materials not found in the logical, objective, real world, such as flying fairies (*Peter Pan*), robots (*R. U. R.*), alternate realities (*The Nether*), or a man with a six-foot-tall, invisible rabbit friend (*Harvey*), but only if action is possible, plausible, and probable within the universe the play creates.

Surprise and mystery are vital components in a play, but not at the expense of the play's own ground rules. For example, unlikely to be plausible, probable, and possible would be a play with a realistic universe that introduces problems that are solved in the last minutes by the surprise appearance of fairies or an invisible rabbit, because they were not part of the play's initial logic.

Plays Are Entertainment

From the first it has been theatre's business to entertain people as it also has been of all the other arts. It is this business which gives it its particular dignity; it needs no other passport but fun.

— Bertolt Brecht

Some scoff at the idea of theatre as entertainment, as if that somehow cheapens the art or makes it into a meringue-filled confection without intellectual substance. In fact, however, to entertain is a respectable and vital aspect of theatre. Those who deny the concept of theatre as entertainment are likely the same people, playwrights and directors, whose theatrical work is self-indulgent, pompous, dull, and noncommunicative, making audiences walk out during performances.

The definitions of "a play" include the audience; the concept of entertainment is a sensible extension of those definitions. A play captures and holds the audience's attention when it entertains, by which is meant "to divert from daily, mundane concerns." It follows that both *King Lear* and *Rent* are entertainment. Both are compelling and well-structured stories that stimulate audiences to concentrate on the action; both are rich in plausible conflict, move toward a future that deeply affects the characters, contain surprise and mystery, have interesting and dimensional characters who face problems that are made significant to their future, contain well-written dialogue, and lift the audience members out of themselves into the universe of the play. As playwrights such as Tom Stoppard have demonstrated, entertaining plays can provoke audiences to respond thoughtfully to important social or other intellectual issues.

Plays Communicate with Emotions

Not all guidelines are acceptable to everyone, and certainly there are several schools of thought regarding the importance of emotion. Some argue that plays communicate to the audience's intellect when emotions are evoked. On the other hand, some echo Plato's belief, later reinforced by Bertolt Brecht's concept of "epic theatre," that audiences stop thinking when in the grips of emotion. (It should be pointed out that even Brecht's plays do use emotional appeal, although he sometimes includes scenes or effects that undercut emotional response.) In any case, wisdom points out that it is senseless to treat emotions and intellect like two unrelated parts of the human response. In fact, they cannot be separated.

Many theatre workers believe that plays are enhanced when characters have reason to experience strong emotions such as love and hate. Without adequate motivation those emotions may degrade to soap opera qualities, but we can safely say that when characters care deeply about the issues and problems they face, the audience also will care, through the process of empathy. Not unimportant for the playwright, actors are apt to become more involved with characters who experience emotional ranges, resulting in powerful interpretations of a play.

Plays Communicate to the Imagination

Producers, directors, actors, and designers seek plays that leap off the page onto the stage, awakening their theatrically trained imaginations to "see" and "hear" the characters and action. Audiences also respond positively to plays that communicate to the imagination, inviting them to participate in the play and empathize with the characters.

Too much detail inhibits imaginative responses, and a primary aspect of playwriting is deciding what to omit or exclude, achieving a balance of mystery with essential clarity. Audiences at a production of *Harvey* readily "see" Harvey through the character's eyes, and the effect would be markedly lessened if a six-foot actor played the role in a bunny suit. Your study of plays such as Harold Pinter's *The Dumbwaiter* and Samuel Beckett's *Waiting for Godot* will help you discover the value of encouraging imaginative response by deciding what *not* to write.

Unities of Time, Place, and Action

The so-called Aristotelian three unities—so-called because they are inaccurately derived from Aristotle's *Poetics*—supposedly require a play to be consistent in time, place, and action. The concept can be confusing because many playwriting textbooks and play directors recommend you follow the unities carefully, but some playwrights and directors tell you to disregard the unities completely. Both extremes have problems.

The unities have a certain logic. Unity of time means that a play's action happens in twenty-four hours or less; unity of place holds the action to a single locale, such as one room; and unity of action (the one unity required by Aristotle) requires the play to dramatize only one central story or action, thus eliminating action not directly relevant to the plot.

These unities often are misunderstood, and we mustn't exaggerate their significance although we must recognize that they can contribute to a play's impact. A playwright has a certain amount of freedom to ignore them, but that freedom isn't absolute. Their importance warrants your study so you can decide when and how to apply the unities to your play.

Historical Obedience to Unities of Time, Place, and Action

Rigid observance of the unities of time, place, and action occurred in various centuries of theatre's development. For one example, Ludovico Castelvetro, the sixteenth-century Italian poet and critic, initiated the concept of "unity of time," basing his conclusions on a passage from Aristotle's *Poetics* that compares epic poetry and tragedy. (The former, Aristotle wrote, can happen over many days, but the latter "endeavors, as far as possible, to confine itself to a single revolution of the sun.")

Castelvetro's concept grew in importance to the point that some Renaissance theorists demanded that "stage time" be congruent with "real time," by which they meant that any real-life action that requires, say, twenty minutes should take precisely the same amount of time onstage. These and comparable rules, known as "neoclassical ideals," permeated much of the Renaissance. Modern theatre, however, is less rigid.

Modern Theatrical Use of the Unities

Today's theatre rejects compulsive observance of the unities on the justifiable grounds that, first, they are based on misreading Aristotle's *Poetics*. Second, portions—not all—of the rules of unities are artificial. Finally, effective contemporary plays prove that the unities are guides, not dictates.

Time and place.   The unities of time and place often are discarded in today's plays, although unity of action continues to be important. Modern use of the unities may be best exemplified by free-flowing plays such as Arthur Miller's *Death of a Salesman*, which moves easily through time and space, most notably with the appearance of Ben, who exists only in Willy's imagination. You can better understand the effect of rigid insistence on unity of time and place by imagining *Salesman* if Miller had confined his play to one time and place. The character of Ben would be eliminated, thus sharply decreasing the portrayal of Willy; and scenes such as Willy with the whore would not be possible, thereby excluding a vital aspect of the Willy–Biff conflict.

Freedom to ignore unities of time and place is accompanied by a need to structure the play tightly, and you must know the chronological order of the action, no matter what unities are shown in the play. We can return to *Salesman* to illustrate this point. Although a casual observer might conclude that Miller's play lacks unification of time because the play shows a number of scenes from Willy Loman's past, in fact *Salesman* has a strong unification of time that is often overlooked: The action deals with the last forty-eight hours of Willy's life.

That observer might say those Willy-Ben or Willy-whore scenes in *Salesman* are flashbacks, but it is more accurate to think of them as insights into moments that are engraved in Willy's mind and make him the man who is dissolving in the present. Miller said his play has no flashbacks but "it is simply that the past keeps flowing into the present, bringing its scenes and its characters with it." Miller didn't distinguish when those moments happened—there's no chronological specificity—but they clearly show young Willy Loman's warped values that lead to his suicide.

Action.   Although modern plays effectively ignore unities of time and place, they usually continue to emphasize unity of action. Without a clear unification of action, plays can be so disconnected that they lose clarity and impact. Certainly *Salesman* has one basic action: Willy's (unsuccessful) efforts to make Biff love him, resulting in his self-destruction.

Unity of action is most important to the playwright. Of the three unities, action is the only one that Aristotle insisted upon and the one that should most concern you. Unity of action, most easily defined as a single, organic plot, is an important structural device to make your play dramatic by maintaining a logical connection between successive events. Unity of action gives strength to such diverse plays as Sam Shepard's *Fool for Love*, Neil Simon's *Broadway Bound*, and Doug Wright's *I Am My Own Wife*.

Advantages of Observing the Unities

Value of the unities.   Although effective plays disregard certain unities, you should recognize the advantages of observing them. One cardinal precept of art is that there must be an underlying unification to the work, a glue that holds all parts together. One technique—certainly not the only way—is through the use of the three unities, and often your play has a stronger chance of being better written, more intense, and stageworthy if you unify time, place, and action. Short monodramas and one-act plays, in particular, usually follow the three unities. Furthermore, observation of the three unities helps you avoid numerous pitfalls lurking to trap the playwright who too freely disregards them; following the unities can help you write more easily.

These advantages do not mean that you must slavishly follow the unities, but they are so significant that beginning playwrights should seriously consider making their first plays unified in time, place, and action. The same advice is valid for advanced writers who have not written a play containing these unities or who are frustrated by problems on a current script.

Tips for Effective Use of the Unities

Plausibility.   Applying a rule of plausibility will help you avoid common pitfalls with time. Avoid calling audience attention to illogical passage of time, such as having a character consume an alcoholic drink on page four and become drunk by page six; sending a character offstage, saying he's going to get a sandwich at the corner deli, only to return with the sandwich on the next page or so; or having an offstage character telephone to say she's on her way over, and then appear onstage within several minutes. Be careful, too, about sending one character offstage to shower or change clothing, which requires a certain passage of time, leaving the other character onstage with nothing to say or do.

Scenery shifts for time or place are distracting.   If you elect to shift time or place during the course of your play, consider making the shifts flow in nonstop action. Stage machinery, no matter how smoothly handled, interrupts the action and disrupts audience concentration. Breaks for scenery shifts to indicate change in time or place are awkward unless done during an intermission.

A careful study of plays that successfully move in time and place will help you better perceive the necessary writing techniques. We've already cited *Salesman* as a model. A second excellent example is *Children of a Lesser God*, a powerful drama by Mark Medoff, which flows freely from scene to scene without interruption or changes in setting. Undoubtedly you can find more.

Some late-twentieth-century and twenty-first-century plays abandon even unity of action. Samples include Lisa Kron's *Well* and Ann Washburn's *Mr. Burns: A Post-electric Play* in which ideas rather than action provide the central unity and David Mamet's one-act *All Men Are Whores* in which scenes are unified by related images. Why would some playwrights completely abandon all three of the traditional unities? Because they are focusing on the fourth unity.

The Fourth (and Most Important) Unity: Playwright's Purpose

Centuries of controversy regarding unities of time, place, and action have overshadowed attention to a more important unification: the playwright's purpose or passion—the spark that gives birth to the writer's germinal idea, the playwright's need to bring to theatrical life a situation, issue, or character that illustrates the writer's deepest inner concerns. Strangely, most playwriting texts ignore unification by playwright's purpose.

Your play will be unified when you know clearly what you want to write and have a definite passion or idea you must communicate. Conversely, plays become murky or confusing when the writer loses sight of the passion that started the writing process. Loss of that vision can result in a play that appears to be two or three plays uncomfortably lumped together.

As you begin thinking of a play that wants to be written, continually ask yourself questions to clarify your goal: "What do I want to say?"

"What ideas or characters do I want to dramatize?" "What's this play all about?" Answers to such questions might be posted on the bulletin board over your writing area, and you may want to glance at them as you first outline and then write your play.

EXERCISES

These exercises will help you think of ways to turn an idea into a stageworthy play. Record answers in your writer's notebook.

1. Go back to the list of stageworthy plays that you compiled after reading the first chapter (or if you didn't write that list, do it now). Write a definition of "a play" that covers all of the plays on that list but that would not include other written materials or performances such as concerts. Check the definitions at the beginning of this chapter. How does your definition compare with them? Consider adding your definition to those by writing it in the margin beside them.

2. Imagine you are commissioned to adapt your favorite novel for the stage. Write an outline of any scenes you wish to include. What changes will you make? In what time and place will you set the action? How will you reduce the number of characters? What will you do to tighten the time? How will you decrease the number of locations? Will you attempt to dramatize the entire novel, or parts? How will you decide? What do you conclude are significant differences between a novel and a play?

3. Select your favorite play and write a brief outline showing how you would make it into a novel.

4. Assume you are commissioned to change your favorite movie into a stage play. Apply the questions from number 2 above to your process. Write a brief outline of any scenes you wish to include. What do you learn about the differences between cinematic and theatrical writing?

5. Turn your attention to a play you want to write. Write a brief synopsis that details the play's conflict. Answer questions such as the following:

   • What does the protagonist want? Be sure that goal is concrete and attainable through active motion. "To find happiness through love," for example, is too abstract, but "to marry Juliet" is playable.

   • Why? What makes that goal important?

   • Why is the protagonist motivated into action now?

   • What obstacles stop him or her from achieving that goal? The longer your play, the more obstacles you'll need. List them in order.

- How does the character respond to those obstacles?
- In your synopsis indicate how the conflicts and action reflect and show the play's content.

6. Write a brief summation of the action and contents of the beginning, middle, and end of the play you want to write.

A play's an interpretation. It is not a report. And that is the beginning of its poetry because, in order to interpret, you have to distort toward a symbolic construction of what happened, and as that distortion takes place, you begin to leave out and overemphasize and consequently deliver up life as a unity rather than as a chaos, and any such attempt, the more intense it is, the more poetic it becomes.

— Arthur Miller

Why do I write at all? There are things that concern me enough to compel the sustained committed effort that leads to the script of a play. I once told a friend in London that my plays are efforts to continue—and perhaps win—certain arguments that I've had with people. And, of course, the plays are about people and relationships—troubled relationships that seem to demand explaining.

— Arnold Wesker

ADDITIONAL READING ON THE TOPICS OF THIS CHAPTER

Castagno, Paul. *New Playwriting Strategies: Language and Media in the 21st Century.* 2nd ed. New York: Routledge, 2012. Ch. 1 "New Playwriting Strategies: Overview and Terms." A "poetics" of new trends in playwriting that lay aside conflict, the unities, and other aspects of traditional dramaturgy.

Vogler, Christopher. *The Writer's Journey: Mythic Structure for Writers.* 3rd ed. Studio City, CA: Michael Wiese Productions, 2007. A clear and simple discussion of the structures that underlie most recent movies as well as numerous plays.

Read some (all?) of the plays mentioned in this chapter. Avoid the temptation to imitate the plays you read, but instead let them set you free to create your own forms that express your "fourth unity." As always, resist the urge to be different just for the sake of being different.

3

The Size of Your Canvas
Monodramas, One-Acts,
and Full-Length Plays

> *Writing has laws of perspective, of light and shade, just as painting does. . . . If you are born knowing them, fine. If not, learn them. Then rearrange the rules to suit yourself.*
>
> — TRUMAN CAPOTE

Playwriting involves filling theatrical time and space, which refers to the length of your script and the action that happens onstage during that period. Length and action match each other—the longer your play, the more complex the action; the smaller the action, the shorter your play—and they combine to attract the audience's attention and awaken its imagination.

Your decisions about time and space are like the painter's choice of canvas size, as large or small as necessary to express your ideas. The painter might start with a vision of a sweeping city scene that demands a huge canvas or even a wall. Or the painter might choose to paint a tiny picture and then select a subject that fits within those confines. Your creative process, like the painter's, includes determining the "dimensions of your canvas," basing your decision on either your play's content or on the length of play you envision.

Determining the Size of Your Canvas

Your canvas may be relatively small, like a brief one-person mono-drama, or increasingly larger, ranging from a one-act to a full-length play. The colors of your canvas evoke the mood you wish—comic, dramatic, or tragic—and you shape the total effect so it communicates to a particular audience that you identify (thinking of age, locale, theatrical sophistication, and so on) at a specific theatre (such as professional, regional, educational, and so forth).

How Do You Decide the Size of Your Play?

You might determine your play's dimensions by first evaluating the scope of your basic germinal image, involving such matters as the complexity of the plot and quantity of incidents, number of characters, physical settings, movement in time or space, and the development of the story. The more complex—the more elbow room you need—the larger your play. Alternatively, you may reverse the process and first select the length and complexity you wish to make your play and then select materials appropriate for that space. A third process, equally valid, is more exploratory: sketching out your play until you discover what size you'll need.

Size of Play Doesn't Equate with Importance

Avoid mistaken concepts that a canvas of a certain size somehow conveys more artistic ability or significance than that of another size, or that "serious" writers tackle only full-length plays because any other size indicates a lack of artistic ambition. Equally, don't let other people push you into those traps, as happened to a promising young playwright who was leaving the theatre following a production of her successful one-act play when a theatre professor said in a patronizing way, "That was nice. But when are you going to write a full-length *real* play?" His narrow-minded question threw her badly off stride, and her writing suffered for several years before she was able to recover her belief in her work.

Protect yourself by vigorously rejecting such poor, even cruel, advice. If you decide to write a short play, keep in mind the opinion of the late Alan Schneider, one of America's outstanding theatrical directors who was responsible for successful Broadway productions of playwrights such as Edward Albee and Samuel Beckett. "I like the short play," he said. "My grandmother taught me that diamonds don't come as large as bricks." Your goal is to select a canvas that expresses your deeply held personal beliefs and vision, following playwright Edward Albee's statement that "it is a playwright's responsibility to reflect and comment on his time as accurately as he possibly can."

The Monodrama

As the name implies, a monodrama is a one-character play. Also known as a theatrical monologue, one-person show, or (in an evocation of vaudeville) a solo turn, it is one of theatre's popular yet, paradoxically, relatively overlooked forms. Monodramas have proven their artistic strengths in professional and amateur productions, yet surprisingly few playwrights think of writing them. The monodrama can be a powerful theatrical work, often using elevated language and powerful images to create poetic enlargement of the character and subject.

Length

The monodrama's playing time can vary from ten minutes to several hours. Short monodramas, highly condensed experiences that make them theatre's equivalent to poetry, often are performed in intimate settings, off- or off-off-Broadway, or regional and amateur theatres. You may write a single monodrama or a collection that can be presented individually or as a group, such as Jane Martin's series of eleven short works under the collective title, *Talking With . . .*

The short monodrama is the smallest theatrical canvas, yet it is a valid artistic form in its own right and can make an exciting theatrical experience for writer, actor, director, and audience. It also will help you improve significant aspects of your playwriting skills such as shaping your play with a beginning, middle, and end; developing rich, dimensional characterization; writing dialogue that is theatrical, concise, and appropriate for the character; expressing your personal vision; and communicating from stage to audience.

Longer monodramas, with playing times equivalent to full-length plays, have had notable successes on Broadway. Examples of modern full-length monodramas include Jay Presson Allen's *Tru,* Jane Wagner's The *Search for Signs of Intelligent Life in the Universe,* and Doug Wright's *I Am My Own Wife.*

A number of full-length monodramas are biographical. For example, monodramas have been written about politicians such as Theodore Roosevelt (*Bully!*) and Harry Truman (*Give 'Em Hell, Harry!*), playwrights such as Tennessee Williams (*Confessions of a Nightingale*) and Lillian Hellman (*Lillian*), and poets such as Emily Dickinson (*The Belle of Amherst*), Edna St. Vincent Millay (*A Lovely Light*), and Gertrude Stein (*Gertrude Stein Gertrude Stein Gertrude Stein*). Autobiographical monodramas, though fewer in number, are also popular, illustrated by Spalding Gray's *Swimming to Cambodia.*

Actors write monodramas to create performance opportunities, as did Hal Holbrook, author of *Mark Twain Tonight!* and Eric Bogosian, who wrote *Drinking in America.* Other monodramas spark actors' careers, such as the *Whoopi Goldberg* monodrama that launched Ms. Goldberg's film successes.

Characteristics of the Monodrama

The monodrama is a flexible form with few apparent rules except the need to entertain in the sense of "enter into," bringing the audience into the world of the character. You capture and hold audience attention with excellent, insightful characterization and carefully selected language that is appropriate to the character.

Number of characters.   Although only one actor is onstage, you can imply the presence of other characters. One effective playwright's technique is to have the character assume the other characters' personalities and voices: Instead of the character saying "Mother always told me that love is merely biological quests . . ." you might write:

> "Mother. Full of advice." (*In the mother's voice, stern, blunt.*) "Chemistry, Jane. Chemistry. That's all there is to love. Hormones, biology, and chemistry. Don't let such foolishness turn your life into chaos." (*Her own voice.*) "Yeah, sure, Mom, that takes care of the magic. Some recipe for relationships. Thanks a helluva lot."

Note that the above technique avoids the past tense: The character's mother is, in effect, talking now, so the character doesn't have to say, "Mother told me. . . ." Samuel Beckett's *Krapp's Last Tape* uses a variation of that approach: The character listens to tape recordings he made to celebrate each birthday.

Dramatic structures.   Monodramas don't always include conflict; you'll find short monodramas that are effective despite the lack of conflict, depending instead on characterization and word choice. But monodramas still utilize other dramatic structures. The central characters of monodramas usually have problems they need to solve or something they need to accomplish. They encounter obstacles to accomplishing their tasks; frequently their biggest obstacles are internal—themselves. They either accomplish their objectives or fail to do so. In failing or succeeding, they change. Their changes include making discoveries about themselves or their world, making decisions, and causing or experiencing changes in their own natures or situations. Most monodramas also have beginnings that set the scene and situation and introduce the characters' goals, middles that develop the story via obstacles and episodes, and endings that conclude the play and depict the changes in the characters or situations.

A fresh insight into the character's world.   Monodramas often conclude with a snap, a piercing insight, such as Jane Martin's *French Fries*, which focuses on an old lady whose major goal is to live at a McDonald's because, she says at the end, "You have to have a dream. Our dreams make us what we are." The play makes the audience think about dreams of living at McDonald's and, by extension, our values within society's fast-food lifestyle.

To Whom Is the Character Speaking?

As you envision your monodrama, you may wonder to whom the person speaks. Why does he or she talk aloud? If possible, simply ignore the question—the character speaks, and that's all there is to it. Still, some playwrights worry about motivation, putting inanimate objects or pets onstage to which the character can speak, but stuffed teddy bears and the like tend to look artificial (and just how many characters would have parrots or goldfish?).

It is better to invent a dynamic character who must speak, is compelled to disclose the inner self, who simply cannot remain silent because of a powerful need to express deeply held beliefs. That approach will help you answer the question, "But to whom does the character speak?" Think of the powerful "Soliloquy" ("My boy Bill") from *Carousel* or "Memories" from *Cats* or "The Story of Jerry and the Dog" from Albee's *The Zoo Story* or "To be or not to be" or any of the other soliloquies that give Shakespeare's characters added dimension.

Some monodramas establish the presence of others onstage. For example, Anna Deavere Smith's Pulitzer Prize nominated *Fires in the Mirror* includes 26 characters. In a slightly different, dialogic approach, Dan O'Brien's *The Body of an American* utilizes two actors who alternate in presenting multiple characters. And Doug Wright's *I Am My Own Wife*, which won both the Pulitzer Prize for Drama and also the Tony Award for Best Play, includes 35 speaking characters, all played by a single male actor wearing a black dress. Performed by talented, experienced actors, such plays intrigue audiences and don't leave them confused.

Strengths and Weaknesses of the Monodrama

The monodrama is to theatre as poetry is to literature—short, clean, a direct penetration of the topic. At its worst, like poor poetry, a monodrama is self-indulgent, wordy because the author fell in love with his or her own voice, too often full of whimpers about failures that are best left hidden in one's diary, and as shapeless as a dirty sock. But like excellent poetry, at its best the monodrama is a shining gem, a glittering and rich illumination of an individual's heart and soul, a compelling story that is carefully shaped with a beginning, middle, and end.

The One-Act Play

Like the theatrical monodrama, the one-act play defies rigid definition; however, if a play of any length has no intermission, it is, technically speaking, a one-act. You'll find one-acts to be flexible, diverse, often experimental, and intensely theatrical. The one-act has an honored tradition: We can say that the early Greek playwrights wrote one-acts, although John

Millington Synge's *Riders to the Sea* is often considered the formal beginning of the modern trend. Many well-known playwrights have written one-acts; some, such as George Bernard Shaw, Eugene O'Neill, Eugène Ionesco, and Edward Albee, started their playwriting careers with one-acts. You'll find excellent one-acts by contemporary playwrights such as Lanford Wilson, Sam Shepard, Joanna Glass, David Mamet, and others. One-acts are popular in high school play festivals or contests, college studio theatres and play direction classes, off- and off-off-Broadway, regional theatre's "second season" productions, and coffeehouses and restaurants.

Length

The one-act, a theatrical version of literature's short story, demands a judicious economy. It typically varies in playing time from perhaps ten minutes to over an hour. Many are around forty minutes long, and there are even tiny, one-minute one-acts. The Actors Theatre of Louisville popularized the ten-minute play, and now there are multiple productions of festivals of ten-minute plays in theatres across the country. At the other end of the spectrum, Jean-Paul Sartre's *No Exit* is close to an hour and a half, illustrating the longer one-act form.

Characteristics of the One-Act

A one-act is like a high-speed photograph of the split-second instant that an object drops into a fluid, causing a diadem of droplets to spray up into the air: From that moment you can infer what the fluid was like before the object struck, the force of the object and what it did to the fluid, where the droplets will go, and what the fluid will become later. The unassisted eye never sees that action. So, too, your one-act is an intensely concentrated moment. The "object" is a conflict. The action implies the whole of the characters' lives, a single incident that sums up their past, present, and future. The audience's eye could not have seen the importance in that moment without your play's guidance. Your goal is to find the moment that encapsulates the characters' lives.

One incident. By definition a one-act is a compressed dramatization of a single incident or sequence of action, unlike a full-length play's expanded multiple incidents or actions. Shakespeare's *Macbeth*, for example, has many incidents; one of them, such as the banquet scene, could be an effective one-act. The one-act often appears at its best when it condenses the action to a single intense moment that implies a past or future, such as Israel Horovitz's *Hopscotch* (which evokes the two characters' history) and John Olive's *Minnesota Moon* (which implies the two characters' future).

Why now? You can structure your one-act (as well as your monodrama and full-length) more effectively if you know why it must take place *now*. Why does it happen today, not yesterday or tomorrow? What makes this particular moment so important? Answers will give your play a greater sense of dramatic urgency.

Number of characters.   The one-act's brevity limits the number of characters, and all must be essential to the play. Too many characters result in thin characterization. A helpful guideline might be to think of two to perhaps four characters. A number of excellent two-character one-acts hold the stage such as *The Zoo Story* by Edward Albee and the previously mentioned *Hopscotch*. Three characters provide good interplay, as in the eternal triangle. If the initial design for your one-act includes more than, say, three or four characters, consider combining several characters into one. Certainly plan to eliminate utilitarian characters who make no major contribution to the action.

Unification.   Effective one-act plays maintain unity of action, focused on one specific event in which a significant change takes place. Unity of place, within a single physical location and unity of time, also help structure these shorter plays. One-acts are so short that a blackout or break in the action to shift scenery or indicate passage of time interrupts the flow, disrupts audience focus on the action, and damages the play's unity. If you find you need several scenes, identify the single crucial scene and ask yourself if the entire play can take place there.

The one-act does not like being confined, however, and you will find variations in form and content. Some effective one-acts move freely through time and space without interrupting the action, such as *Pvt. Wars* by James McLure and *Canadian Gothic* by Joana Glass. A few others call for blackouts to indicate changes in time and space, such as *The Dance and the Railroad* by David Henry Hwang.

Strengths and Weaknesses of the One-Act

At its worst, the one-act falls victim to its experimental nature, seeking merely to be different (forgetting that originality does not necessarily equal quality) and ignoring commonsense structural elements. But the one-act is at its best when sharply focused on a single significant incident, with excellent characterization and a story that is compressed into its essentials. One-acts are carefully edited with a keen sense of theatre to eliminate unnecessary words and action. Freedom to explore new forms often creates exciting theatre, and the one-act provides a great opportunity for such innovations.

The Full-Length Play

Is your idea a mural that requires a number of actions or incidents to show the play's theme and conflicts, the development of an involved story, complex character evolution and change, and possibly movement in time and space? If so, you're probably thinking of a full-length play, theatre's largest and most complicated form. Like the novel, the full-length must have contents that demand enlarged size.

Length

The full-length play provides an evening's entertainment, usually one and a half to two and a half hours of playing time. As you would expect, some playwrights defy the conventional length, notably Eugene O'Neill, whose *Mourning Becomes Electra* and *Strange Interlude* are each five hours long, and David Edgar, whose adaptation of Charles Dickens's novel, *The Life and Adventures of Nicholas Nickleby*, ran eight and one half hours. Audiences for these long plays arrive at the theatre in the afternoon, leave for dinner at an intermission, then return to see the rest of the play. Those exceptions aside, however, most full-length plays offer less extended entertainment.

Characteristics of the Full-Length Play

Think of your full-length play as a story so rich in detail that it demands full-length treatment. One guideline is to be sure your full-length play simply cannot be told in shorter form. For example, we can't imagine effective short versions of plays such as Charles Fuller's *A Soldier's Play*, Beth Henley's *Crimes of the Heart*, or Lorraine Hansberry's *A Raisin in the Sun*, which all have a scope that demands full-scale expression. Avoid trying to make a full-length by adding scenes to what should be a short play; such padding will only weaken your writing.

Number of acts.   An act, the portion of a play taking place between intermissions, is the largest division of your script, consisting of a unified group of activities and containing smaller divisions such as beats, segments, and scenes. Modern full-length plays are two or three acts, with the two-act structure more popular because one less interruption permits the playwright to make the action more intense. The five-act form, once standard, is out of style, and a four-act form never materialized.

Conflict.   Your full-length is likely to have one major through-line conflict, typically involving a protagonist fighting to achieve a goal against determined opposition. The conflict starts early at the point of attack, is continually refreshed and refocused with complications, and finally reaches its peak at the climax. The protagonist succeeds or loses. Secondary conflicts, usually lasting for only a scene or two, are directly related to that single basic struggle. Longer secondary conflicts may be *substories*.

Incidents.   Unlike the one-act, full-length plays have more than a single incident. Shakespeare's plays, for example, tend to have some twenty-five or so incidents. No one can state just how many incidents are necessary to sustain the full-length because some playwrights create brief incidents, and therefore will have more in their plays, while others write elongated incidents, requiring fewer to develop the story and hold audience attention. Comedies typically have more incidents than dramas or tragedies.

Most full-length plays also have more characters than one-acts, but the economics of many theatres suggest that non-musical plays that demand more than eight actors may have difficulty finding productions. If necessary to develop your story, full-length plays can change time and place. Such shifts may occur at any time during the play; however, changes demanding the moving of scenery can severely impact the progress of the action and are therefore best done during intermissions.

Strengths and Weaknesses of the Full-Length Play

At their worst, a full-length play can wander without shape, forgetting that economical statement is as essential as in short plays. And some start with fire but lose strength in the second half because the conflict can't sustain the effort. But at their best, full-length plays are powerful communications that pull the audience into a new world, bringing delight and wonderment. Their length allows a broad, sweeping canvas, and can deeply impact audiences.

Thinking of Audiences and Types of Theatres for Your Play

Regardless of the size of your canvas, your first goal is to write a play that satisfies you. It must be true to itself. In this sense you write for yourself. But being a playwright also requires thinking of your play's audience, represented by the sort of theatrical organization you hope will produce your play. Think of appealing to that ideal theatre's various strengths, economic conditions, artistic goals, acting and directing skills, and especially its audience, whether young people or adults, in religious or secular settings. These considerations impact such matters as cast size and production values (scenery, lighting, costumes, properties, sound, and so forth). They also may influence your choice of dialogue and action, based on your awareness that some audiences may object to what is euphemistically called "adult language and situations."

What Theatres Present Monodramas and One-Act Plays?

Short plays, such as monodramas and one-acts, typically are presented by small, intimate theatres and workshops, especially in regional and off- and off-off-Broadway theatres. The short play is particularly popular in educational theatres: College students present one-acts in studio theatres as part of their directing class assignments, and high schools present one-acts in contests or festivals. Your play will receive earnest and thorough directing and acting in such theatres, but they seldom can afford complicated or expensive production values. Scripts demanding full-scale production values, such as elaborate sets, usually are rejected by such theatres.

Collections of unified one-acts, such as Robert Anderson's *I Never Sang for My Father* and Neil Simon's *Plaza Suite*, have been presented on Broadway and treated as full-length plays. Often the individual units are popular in college studio theatres.

What Theatres Present Full-Length Plays?

Full-length plays are standard fare for Broadway and regional professional theatres, as well as community, dinner, and educational theatres. These productions usually are well financed and are mounted on well-equipped stages. Full-length plays therefore tend to receive lavish sets, scenery, costumes, and lighting. Nonetheless, playwrights writing for Broadway or professional theatres are advised to consider production costs, calling for only one set and relatively few performers. Educational theatres, on the other hand, often search for large-cast plays and are not reluctant to use complex production values.

EXERCISES

1. Examine a monodrama, one-act, and full-length play, perhaps choosing from plays referenced in this chapter. Other than length, what differences do you see? What similarities?

2. Write a brief outline of each of those plays, describing the action. What happened before the play began (the establishing event)? What sparks the conflict (the point of attack)? What does the protagonist want? What obstacles are in his or her path?

3. Shape a brief outline of a monodrama you might write. Assume it will be short, perhaps with a playing time of ten minutes. Although monodramas can succeed without conflict, think of a character with a powerful goal that is opposed by an equally powerful force. Describe the character's major emotions. What does he or she want? Why? What obstacles prevent the character from achieving that goal?

4. Build a brief outline of a one-act you might write. Assume you'll have not more than three or four characters and that all action happens in one time and place. Start the one-act in the middle of ongoing action (*in medias res*), and let background information (exposition) come later when it sparks the action.

5. Construct a brief outline of a full-length play you might write. Be sure all action happens now, not in the past, and drives toward a

future. Who is the protagonist? What does he or she want? Why? How strongly? Who opposes his or her goal? List the events in order. Don't worry about act divisions yet; instead, think primarily of each scene of action. To help you better understand the action, try giving each scene a descriptive title that indicates what happens.

A commercial painter paints flat; you can put your finger through. But a painter—for example, an apple by Cézanne has weight. And it has juice, everything, with just three strokes. I tried to give my words just the weight that a stroke of Cézanne's gave to an apple. That is why most of the time I use concrete words. . . . I think what the critics call my "atmosphere" is nothing but the impressionism of the painter adapted to literature.

— Georges Simenon

ADDITIONAL READING ON THE TOPICS OF THIS CHAPTER

Ansell, Steve and Rose Burnett Bonczek. *One Minute Plays: A Practical Guide to Tiny Theatre.* Routledge, 2017. An anthology of 200 1-minute plays plus a guide to writing them, staging one-minute-play festivals, etc.

Garrison, Gary. *A More Perfect Ten: Writing and Producing the 10-Minute Play.* Focus, 2009. A wise and witty guide by a master of the form.

Kearns, Michael. *Getting Your Solo Act Together.* Heinemann, 1997. How to write, produce, and evaluate monodramas in the Spalding Gray, personal narrative mode.

4

Where Do You Start?
Turning Your Vision into Plays

> *I can't even count how many times I've heard the line, "Where did the idea for this play come from?" I never can answer it because it seems totally back-assward. Ideas emerge from plays—not the other way around.*
>
> — SAM SHEPARD
>
> *You have to find the story; you can't just set out to write a play about politics or it would be as boring as hell.*
>
> — J. T. ROGERS

A dedicated writer's lavish expenditure of time and energy could bewilder an efficiency expert. Even your friends and family may wonder what takes you so long to get your play going; isn't writing merely a matter of putting down your ideas?

Well, no. Seldom is it that simple.

Although outsiders may believe writers start with a complete vision of what they'll create and then simply follow that path, being a playwright is more a process of search, exploration, and discovery. Certainly it is efficient to begin with a clear knowledge of all aspects of your play, but often you must write to find what you want to write, encountering new ideas through writing, confronting what you believe as you write, focusing your thoughts and making choices, and always thinking of writing to make your ideas come to life through the alchemy of the theatre.

Plays seldom jump full-blown into existence but instead are products of the logical and creative investigation of ideas. Creativity is one half of a pair of scissors. The other half is perseverance, a willingness to work through your ideas, one step at a time if necessary. Often those apparently small steps will suddenly give you large leaps forward. The scissors are kept sharp by a positive "Yes, I can!" attitude, faith in yourself and your ability to succeed, even though you won't do it all at once.

Avoid frustration by expecting too much of yourself—it's a mistake to think that if you were somehow "really creative" you'd conceive the total play quickly or easily, and you're setting yourself up for disappointment if you expect some magical flash of inspiration to give you a full-scale play. Despite poets' flowery descriptions, there is no creative muse who waves a magic wand so—poof!—you have written a play. Experienced writers will tell you that creativity is one-tenth inspiration and nine-tenths perspiration.

What are the sources of images for plays? How do you use them? How can you flesh them out? In this chapter we begin discussions of transforming ideas into plays; later chapters focus more specifically on theatrical elements such as character, plot, and dialogue.

Sources of Plays: Germinal Images

First, what are you looking for? You're looking for the seed that will grow into the full-flowering plant that will be your play. This seed needs to be appropriate to drama; if you want to grow a watermelon, you don't plant corn. So what kind of seed is likely to grow a play? Remember that you're aiming for a finished product that will capture and share human experience. You're not aiming to write an essay; you're aiming to write a play. As Sam Shepard's epigram at the beginning of this chapter suggests, a propositional idea is more suitable for an essay than as the seed for a play. So what shall we call this seed? Maybe, *vision*? That seems too nebulous, too broad; we need something specific. How about *image*? An image is a mental picture of a person, object, or situation. We can include the seed analogy if we call this start of your play a *germinal image*.

Since the germinal image must catch your attention and pull you into developing and writing the play, it will necessarily be suited to you as an individual. We'll consider several types of germinal images here as samples.

Starting with a Situation

If you're thinking of actions or things happening, perhaps physical or psychological events, predicaments, and emergencies, your initial idea is a situation. You might wonder, for instance, "What happens to people when they are trapped in a tense physical situation that threatens their personal security or even their lives? How do they react? Most of us think we're fairly civilized beings, but what happens to our veneer of civilization when we face a major crisis?" Perhaps you add insight by asking, "What would I do if intruders came into my home? Would I protect myself and my family? How?" Here you are thinking primarily of people facing a series of crises.

Write down the situation.   As you think of "what happens," be as specific as you can. Picture the details. Remember—we're after an image. Who's there? What are they doing? How are they relating? What has just happened or about to happen? What colors do you see? What do you hear? What odors are the people smelling? Write your germinal situation down in a brief paragraph.

Starting with Character

If your germinal idea is a fictional, real, or historical person, you're beginning with character. Likely you hear and see selected aspects of the character in your imagination, although you may not yet know the details that surround those glimpses. For example, perhaps you're fascinated by the character of Abraham Lincoln. You might wonder, "What was the source of Lincoln's greatness? How did Lincoln cope with what he saw as his countless defeats? What was the essence of his inner strength that helped him overcome depression so he became president?" Your interest is human psychology, the workings of the psyche, a specific human's emotional and intellectual reactions to major difficulties.

Write a description of your character.   As you visualize this character, you'll discover the kinds of details you notice when you first meet a very interesting person. Write down these observations. Also write down what you hear and see the character saying and doing. It may be too early to write a full character description, but record those first impressions. Again, focus on imagistic observations—things that you would note about the character with your senses of sight, hearing, touch, maybe even smell. And note a couple things about the character's personality, hopes, and fears.

Starting with a Place

If your imagination is piqued by a specific location that seems to be just waiting for something memorable to happen there, you're beginning with a place. It might be a secret place that you would go to as a child when you wanted to be alone. Or it might be a forest glen you passed through on a hike that seemed spookily alive. Or it might be a machine shop where you worked part-time while going to school, a grimy place fraught with noises, dangerous machinery, and workers balancing their jobs with their outside lives. Some types of places have been so often used as settings for plays that they have become clichés; do we really need another play that takes place on a park bench? Maybe we do; maybe your play will convert that park bench into a paradise or an inferno.

Write a description of your place. Close your eyes and mentally enter your germinal space. Use all your senses to notice how the place feels, looks, sounds, and smells. Use your extrasensory perceptions to note the character of the place, what events from the past have made it what it is, what possibilities it holds for affecting people who will enter it. Write down these details in a brief paragraph.

Starting with a Subject

If your germinal idea is an issue that grips you, you're starting with a subject or topic. Myriad issues enliven the Internet, fill the newspapers, and fuel hours of programming on CNN. Some of these no doubt arouse your interests and your passion, and you may want to address them in a play. Remember that you are writing a play, not a sermon, not a political speech, not a debate. Of course there are didactic plays and movies that express strong viewpoints and are intended to inform, convince, or move to action. Samples include the medieval *Everyman* and Clifford Odets's *Waiting for Lefty*. But audiences tend to be more deeply moved by plays that, without taking an argumentative position, powerfully depict people caught up in issues. Samples of this kind of play include Arthur Miller's *The Crucible*, Tony Kushner's *Angels in America*, and Lucas Hnath's *The Christians*.

Write your ideas about your subject. Unless you want to write a dramatic rant, you will do well to jot down viewpoints on *all* sides of the issue that intrigues you—including viewpoints you do not personally share. And then seek a story—in other words, a set of characters in a situation that forces them to face your germinal issue. As J. T. Rogers, author of the Tony-winning play *Oslo*, wrote in the epigram at the beginning of this chapter, "You have to find the story." Your job as a playwright, then, will be to tell the story truly. So write a brief paragraph that sketches out who these characters are and what situation they face.

Working with Your Germinal Images

A writer's creative ideas are like flashes of lightning bugs on a warm summer evening. They flick on unexpectedly and then move away, temporary glimmers of light that are difficult to catch. Being a playwright requires capturing each insight, whether large or small, so you can use it in your play.

Avoid Judgmental Conclusions about Your Initial Idea

Criticizing your initial idea is a negative habit that will put you in a deadly frozen state, stopping the flow of creative impulses. The glimmer of light disappears. Not every idea will evolve into a play, but avoid jumping to conclusions such as "That's not good enough," "This idea is dumb," or "That won't work." You can't know the value of the idea until you work it over, weigh it, think of its shape, ask what elements you can add or changes you might make, and consider options and possibilities.

Even when you can't immediately find a place for the idea, preserve it carefully so it can germinate. Your subconscious can work on it and you, like many other playwrights, may find later that you suddenly have a vision for a play. That flash of insight isn't sudden, of course; it started months earlier when you had an idea that you saved in your writer's notebook, and your subconscious mind was working it over for a long time before you became aware that the idea had grown and evolved.

Avoid a Quest for "Originality"

Deliberately trying to be original is as dangerous as making judgmental conclusions about ideas for plays. A quest for originality is a false priority that will make you dismiss otherwise valid concepts, and the more you try to be somehow novel or different, the more likely your play will be trendy but lack genuine substance. Avoid artificial evaluative standards about your ideas such as "This isn't different enough," "Oh, no, that's been done before," or "But this won't prove to others that I've got a really creative mind." Your personal input into that germinal seed, your insertion of *self*, is the true mark of originality.

Record Germinal Ideas in Your Writer's Notebook

Regardless of the size or detail of your original idea, discipline yourself to capture it immediately by writing it in your writer's notebook, preserving it for future use. Saying, "Oh, sure, I'll remember it" leads to loss of ideas: You'll forget more than you retain. More significantly, the act of writing enhances ideas and creates fresh insights, and you'll discover that writing all ideas that come to you will encourage your subconscious to continue feeding ideas to you.

Being a playwright means writing; recording your ideas in your notebook is an excellent step toward that goal. Fragments of dialogue, interesting characters, puzzling situations, intriguing stories in newspapers or magazines—all of these and more will give you glimmers of ideas for plays and therefore belong in your writer's notebook.

Keep your writer's notebook with you at all times to record ideas the moment they occur. You'll find you're building a rich treasure chest of creative impulses, thoughts, and ideas about situation, character, and topic. These will help you with the play you're now writing and give you materials for future works.

Keep Your Images to Yourself

Although you will be sorely tempted to tell the world about your terrific idea for that Pulitzer Prize winning play, at this point you need to keep it to yourself. There are two reasons to keep it quiet. First, this tender seed, exciting as it is to you, is vulnerable. All you will need from a trusted friend or lover is a look that says, "Well, that's a dumb idea that'll never work!" and your germinal image will wither and die. Best not share it until you've developed it much further and its vigor has turned it into a sapling that can weather a storm of doubts. The second reason to keep it to yourself is that you need to pour your energies into nurturing the idea. Don't fritter away that energy describing your image. So when your friends ask you if you're working on a play, and you're tempted to tell them about your germinal image, resist! Just say, "Oh, yeah, and it's a beauty, but I can't talk about it yet." You'll drive 'em crazy. Then go to work fleshing out your image.

Fleshing Out Germinal Images

In addition to not talking about your play idea too soon, resist two other temptations. Do not immediately begin writing the first scene. Although your germinal image excites you and stimulates all kinds of energy, it's not well enough developed yet to sustain the hard work of writing the dialogue. Playwrights who immediately jump on an idea and begin drafting dialogue are likely to have a whole drawer full of the first scenes of aborted plays that died because their seed ideas weren't well enough developed. Secondly, don't push the development of your image too hard. A gardener who scoops large quantities of root stimulator on a new plant will end up the next day with a dead stick. Wise gardeners know how to gently nurture seedlings with judicious amounts of water and food. So work daily on developing that new idea, but discipline yourself to give it a little work each day. You'll find that the time you spend away from it will contribute to its growth.

Nurturing Your Germinal Image

Some playwrights love the process of developing their script ideas. Tony Kushner said that he so loves research and so dreads drafting dialogue that he limits his research for a new play to one year. Whether you share this love for research or just can hardly wait to start writing dialogue, your play is likely to profit from nurturing that germinal image. Some call this process making a collection, some call it research, and some call it inventing; each of those terms indicates parts of the development process. You might think of this process in terms of locations where you will pursue it.

In the library or online.   Yes, some of the playwright's developmental work can best be done in the library, or online. You may want to read some books related to your topic area. You may use search engines on your computer to increase your acquaintance with aspects of your play. The point is not to turn you into a scholar or to make your play more erudite; the point is to increase your background knowledge of matters related to your play.

On-site.   Where can you go to learn more about the play you are developing? Examples abound of playwrights who travelled across the country or around the world to interview people or experience locations they are writing about. While your budget and schedule may not support international travel, there are likely to be places and people in your own locality that can contribute much to your play. If one of your characters is physically ill or mentally disturbed, consider interviewing a doctor or nurse in your acquaintance. If, as suggested earlier in this chapter, your play is set in a machine shop, pay a visit to such a business and ask if you can observe activities for a day. If you are writing about a homeless person, eat a few meals at a soup kitchen. The notes you make about what you observe will prove very useful as you write your play, but more than that, the act of putting your body in unfamiliar places will give your writing a depth it will get no other way.

At your desk.   Some of your developmental work will be done at your desk, your computer, the coffee shop table, or wherever it is that you most productively work. This activity will permit making notes from your reading and on-site visits and will also include time thinking and inventing. Give a desk session to listing a page full of title ideas for your play. Give another session to sketching out possible characters to include. Use the materials in this book's chapters on plot, character, diction, and production elements to further develop your thoughts about your script. And give several sessions to dealing with the questions that follow at the end of this chapter.

Keep notes of all the insights you gather from on-site visits, reading, and desk work. Eventually, you are likely to find yourself beginning to write down snatches of dialogue. That may be an indication that it's time to move on to drafting dialogue. If you've done your collection work well, you'll find that the dialogue writing will be a joy and that your play will be rich with detail.

In the acting studio.   Some playwrights, like Megan Terry and Caryl Churchill, have developed plays in collaboration with actors. Once your ideas have developed far enough that you can share them with others, and if you have actor friends who are willing to help you develop your play, you might work with them. One approach would be to suggest a situation to the actors, give them a few details about each of their characters, and then ask them to improvise a scene in which the characters work through the given situation. They will likely have used similar techniques in their training as well as when rehearsing specific plays. Their approaches to the exercise may suggest things you had not previously imagined about the characters or their situation.

Alternatively, you might explore your characters or situations using the Stanislavskian acting technique called the "magic if." This approach involves asking a series of "what if" questions. An actor cast as Macbeth, for instance, may develop his character by asking "What if I were alive centuries ago: What would I feel and do if I suddenly encountered the 'weird sisters' who promised I would become king?" Note that the question doesn't encourage the actor to think what *he* would do in those circumstances; instead, it puts him into the character's world. You or your actor friends might use similar creative "what if" questions to help develop your situations and characters. Asking such questions stimulates your creativity, prompts your subconscious to think of solutions, and helps you see more deeply into the characters and possible alternative ways of bringing them to life.

Developing Your Idea's Theatrical Potential

If I didn't know the ending of a story, I wouldn't begin. I always write my last lines, my last paragraph, my last pages first, and then I go back and work toward it. I know where I'm going. I know what my goal is. And how I get there is God's grace.

— Katherine Anne Porter

I think the theatre should try to be emotional, colorful. I think everybody's tired of stages where nothing happens. The theatre is the art of the emotions—it is also that of the concrete.

— Boris Pasternak

The following questions can help you develop your germinal images. Later chapters will amplify these concepts.

What Might Be the Play's Major Conflicts?

Drama usually requires force against force, a battle for survival, whether physical, psychic, or psychological. What conflicts are suggested by your germinal image? Is the conflict a result of the central character's basic desire? How might you sustain the conflict throughout your play? How could you *show* the conflict instead of just *telling* about it?

Whose Play Is It?

Who is the central character? How will he or she remain active throughout the play? What strong goal might the central character pursue during the play? What motivates that character to pursue that goal? What might the character have at stake—what will be lost if he or she doesn't achieve that goal? What qualities might make this character engaging for the audience?

Who Might Be the Secondary Characters, and What Might Make Them Interesting?

Identify some potential major players in the action. What are their emotions, hopes, dreams, relationships? What might these secondary characters have at stake? What is their emotional investment in the outcome? How might you develop them to give them playable dimensions and emotions that actors can bring to life?

How Might You Structure Your Play?

What might happen in your play? How might it begin? How might it end? Can you list things that might happen between beginning and end? What are some obstacles and complications that might sustain and heighten the action?

What Production Values Might Your Play Have?

Where does the play take place, and what kind of set do you envision? Even though the designers will create the actual sets, lights, and costumes, what kind of visual elements do you imagine? What kinds of sound might help communicate the play? What theatrical devices might you use—things like projections, direct audience address, poetic dialogue, character doubling, special effects, etc.

What Forms Might Best Fit Your Play?

How would your play work as a comedy? As a tragedy? As a drama? As a dramedy? Before you plunk down hard for one of these modes, imagine the play as each of them. This can be an especially useful exercise if you have immediately (for instance) pictured your play as a tragedy. Consider how you might make it a comedy. You might find that it would be even more effective as a dark comedy, or as a tragedy with comic elements.

Again, How Might Your Play Begin?

This question is not just about what happens first in your play. It's also about the *moment* you will depict. What might be the most important moments in the lives of your characters, the moments that will bring their whole lives into focus? Sophocles, for instance chose two different moments for his two plays about Oedipus—the day he discovered his true identity (*Oedipus the King*) and the day of his death (*Oedipus at Colonus*).

Do You Know How the Action Ends?

Not all writers echo Katherine Anne Porter's statement that she must write the ending before the beginning of her story. Many writers say they start at the beginning without knowing where things will go. Regardless of your approach, at this early planning stage, ask yourself how your play might conclude in a way that would be unexpected but still believable. Endings are crucial. As Richard Krevolin says in *How to Adapt Anything into a Screenplay*, a film's ending has a great deal to do with what the movie means and what lasting effect it will have on its audience. This principle is just as true for stage plays, so imagine several ways your script might end.

EXERCISES

Take your time working through these exercises. File your notes in appropriate locations in your writer's notebook.

1. Write a situation you would like to turn into a play. First describe the situation in one paragraph. Then ask yourself what interests you about the situation? What starts the action? Why? What happens? What are the major incidents? How does the action end? Put the events into a logical order. Describe the characters who would be involved.

2. Write about the central character you'd like to have in a play. Why does this character interest you? What does he or she want? What are the character's major emotions? What crucial moments have punctuated the character's life? After you've finished identifying the character, write details about situations that would show aspects of the character you think are most significant. What other characters would be necessary to bring that character to life?

3. Write about a topic or subject that is important to you and that you'd like to make the core of a play. Why does it interest you? What makes it important? Define what it means to you. After you've finished describing the topic, imagine details about the people who would bring it to life by their actions. Describe a situation in which the characters would live.

4. Of the three germinal ideas above, which works best for you? Amplify the idea in detail. Translate the idea into actions that show what you want audiences to see and feel.

In creating, the only hard thing's to begin; A grass blade's no easier to make than an oak.

— James Russell Lowell

A writer needs three things, experience, observation, and imagination, any two of which, at times any one of which, can supply the lack of the others.

— William Faulkner

ADDITIONAL READING ON THE TOPICS OF THIS CHAPTER

Krevolin, Richard. *How to Adapt Anything into a Screenplay.* Wiley, 2003. Ch. 2 "Professor K.'s Five-Step Adaptation Process." Although focused on cinema writing, this chapter has useful ideas that can be used in planning play scripts.

Neipris, Janet. *To Be a Playwright.* Routledge, 2005. Ch. 3 "Fifty Questions to Ask When Writing a Play." An extensive agenda of questions to use to develop your script.

Smiley, Sam with Norman A. Bert. *Playwriting: The Structure of Action.* 2nd ed. Yale University Press, 2005. Ch. 2 "Finding and Developing Ideas." A step-by-step guide for beginning work on a play.

5

Building Plot
Shaping Your Play's Action

> *On balance, I feel I did crafted work in my first piece* [Five Finger Exercise]. *It said what I wanted it to say, and it possessed a shape which made it play easily and finally accumulated its power. This quality of shape it very important to me. I have always entertained the profoundest respect for art, meaning "artifact," and for the suffix "wright" in the word playwright. I hope* [my plays] *are wrought properly and that they proclaim this fact sufficiently to give* [the] *audience a deep satisfaction in their form and their finish. I also hope that these qualities are not too assertively evident—because if a play irritates by seeming to be too well made, this surely means that it has not been well made enough: that smoothness of the joinery is sealing the work off from the viewer.*
>
> — PETER SHAFFER

Character, or plot—which one should you think of first when you start to plan your play? Which is more important to make a good play?

Aware that playwriting is an art that attracts creative writers with firm convictions, you won't be surprised to discover that questions involving the supremacy of character versus plot will produce two diametrically opposed beliefs held by equally fervent supporters. One suspects that a poll of playwrights would reveal a fifty-fifty schism of opinions about the relative importance of character or plot.

Some playwrights say emphatically that the structure of action is the most important element in a play; audiences are interested in what happens in a play—and therefore you should focus on plotting your play before considering character. After all, the plot unifies your play.

Others, just as emphatic, say that character is more important than plot—audiences are interested in the people of a play—and you should first establish your play's characters before considering its structure. After all, characters unify your play.

Clearly, given the wide differences of opinion, neither extreme is correct. Or both are. Although for the purposes of discussion here, we necessarily must discuss character and plot separately, in fact they are two halves of a whole, and an accurate description of the importance of these two elements can be stated simply: Plot is character in action.

This chapter on plot may strike you as a mechanical, perhaps even arbitrary, maybe formulaic approach to playwriting. Certainly plot can be complicated with cogs and gears and wheels within wheels, operating like a well-oiled piece of machinery to move the play in its inexorable build to the future, and the following discussion of plot's typical elements will focus on each piece.

Most plays include all or most of the elements described below. They provide the basic building blocks of dramatic plots. Study them, look for and identify them in plays you read or see, and learn to use them in your own writing. Becoming a playwright means, in part, gaining the skills to fashion effective plots and understanding how the various parts fit together to impact an audience.

The order in which we will discuss these parts comes from traditional dramaturgy that was based on Aristotle's *Poetics* and was subsequently developed and refined throughout dramatic history. However, many plays, especially many written since the middle of the twentieth century, omit some of the elements and rearrange the rest. Many plays—especially those in the well-made play or realistic traditions like *A Doll's House* or *A Streetcar Named Desire*—conceal the workings of their plots while nevertheless utilizing all of these elements. Other plays, like Lisa Kron's *Well*, spotlight and even overtly question dramatic plot structures. In short, there are no rules for plotting; each playwright must devise the best plot for each play. The process is exciting. Learn to enjoy it.

Three Basic Divisions of Plot

Plot is the master design of the play's conflicts, the selection and arrangement of incidents to achieve maximum impact, and an organized development of the story in a way that fits your play's particular demands. Since every play presents selected materials in a specified order, all plays have plots; there is no such thing as a play without a plot. Of course, plays can have weak plots, confusing plots, ineffective plots, or overly predictable plots. But an effective plot keeps the play moving forward, makes a compelling story that enriches characterization, shows the play's theme in action, and creates suspense and mystery to grip the audience's attention.

Most plots can be subdivided into three basic parts. Part One, the beginning, is introductory material, which establishes the play's initial sense of equilibrium and contains such storytelling devices as exposition and foreshadowing. Part Two, the play's middle, contains the protagonist's goal, discovery, complications and reversals, and the like, and continues up to the play's climax. Part Three, the ending, resolves the play's issues and restores a sense of balance in the play's universe.

Length of Each Part

The beginning, middle, and end are equally important, but they are not equally long. At the risk of being arbitrary, we can indicate general lengths for each part, understanding that your particular play may demand a different form.

Full-length play. Assuming a full-length play around 110 manuscript pages, the beginning is relatively brief, perhaps 5 to 15 pages. The middle contains the major action of the play and therefore is the longest, around 85 to 100 pages. The ending is rather short, around 5 to 10 pages.

One-act play. The one-act typically has proportionally shorter beginning and ending portions. For a 40-page script, the beginning might be 1 to 3 pages, the middle approximately 33 to 38 pages, and the ending around 1 to 4 pages.

These lengths are approximations and must not be followed slavishly, but they do suggest the relative development of each part. Note the brevity of the beginning, indicating that a play should get to the action as soon as possible.

A Typical Sequence of a Plot's Elements

The following discussion addresses each element in the order it typically occurs in a traditionally structured play. Not all plays follow this model, but a careful study of dramatic literature will show you that a surprisingly large percentage of plays—even many considered nontraditional or experimental—use this basic sequence of elements.

Part One: Beginning—Introductory Materials

We live in what is, but we find a thousand ways not to face it. Great theatre strengthens our faculty to face it.

— Thornton Wilder

The first section of your play introduces the audience to the characters, the situation, and the environment. It includes hints or warnings of forthcoming events. These introductory materials, although important to bring the audience into the play's particular universe, should be kept relatively brief.

Design your play's beginning by deciding at what point events must be shown. Three criteria help you select the appropriate moment for your play to begin:

- No earlier portions of the story are necessary for the play's action to develop.

- No additional events are necessary to start the action.

- Start close to the action, even in the middle of ongoing action, to get preliminaries out of the way relatively quickly so you can move to the more active part of your play.

Think of your story in a timeline continuum from the first moment to the final event. To visualize the narrative that underlies your play, try drawing a long line on a sheet of paper. Let the line represent time. Mark all incidents that make up the past, present, and future of your characters in chronological order, from beginning to end.

To find the moment that best begins your play, look for the incident on that line which will spark the action and start a series of complications that leads to the climax. For example, Tennessee Williams could have selected any number of points along the line to begin *A Streetcar Named Desire:* Blanche trying to hold Belle Reve together, Blanche dealing with a death at Belle Reve, Blanche with the traveling salesmen at the Hotel Flamingo in Laurel, or even Blanche already at the Kowalski home and having lived there for several months. Any of those points would have told the basic story, but only one beginning meets the three criteria above: The play's beginning starts moments before Blanche arrives at the Kowalskis' because the plot's conflict begins with the initial encounter between Stanley and Blanche. All earlier events, although important, are not necessary for the play's action.

Establishing Event

The establishing event is a major occurrence that happened before your play began, that is, before the curtain rises on your play. Typically the characters do not yet know the full significance of that event, but relatively soon after the play begins they will discover its relevance to their lives. In *Hamlet*, for example, the establishing event is the combination of the death of Hamlet's father and his mother's remarriage to Claudius; Hamlet discovers the importance of that incident when the Ghost appears. The establishing event will be linked to the point of attack and told to the audience with exposition.

What's the advantage of the establishing event?   A strong establishing event gets your play off to a richly dramatic start and eases your writing process. It will strengthen the point of attack and the protagonist's motivation to drive for a goal, which in turn will help you see subsequent action with complications and reversals. Importantly, the establishing event helps you keep a clear focus on your play's design and gives directors significant insight into your plot.

Must I be sure that the establishing event is clear?   Most playwrights would answer, "Yes, at least in the author's mind." A study of plays will show you that it is usually quite clear to the audience. On the other hand, playwrights such as Harold Pinter communicate satisfactorily without a specific establishing event, using, instead, vaguely implied conditions. Full-length plays typically are based on a major establishing event, although some one-act plays and short monodramas appear to lack one.

State of Equilibrium

Plays usually start with a state of equilibrium depicted in the very first scene. Some experts call this scene the play's balance or stasis. Forces may be aligned equally, or they might be uncomfortably unbalanced but nevertheless at rest. *Hamlet* and *Death of a Salesman*, for example, begin with a skewed balance—things are not right in the play's world—but nonetheless there is a static balance. Although nothing has really happened yet during the balance, it frequently includes several elements that prepare for the play's action—exposition, foreshadowing, and expression of the play's basic mood.

Exposition

Exposition gives the audience background information regarding the situation, characters, relationships, time and place of the action, and the like. Exposition during the first scene is especially likely to clarify the establishing event. You'll find blatantly obvious exposition in older plays, sometimes delivered by a narrator or a pair of servants. Approximately the first third of Euripides's *Medea*, for example, is heavily laden with exposition delivered by the Nurse, the Chorus, and the Attendant. Some more recent plays have equally conspicuous exposition, using artificial devices such as messages from the radio, television, or telephone. Few directors appreciate scripts with such obvious exposition, and your play has a better chance of being accepted if you develop techniques to disguise exposition.

What's the most effective way to use exposition?   Craft exposition so it is subtle; exposition is best when not recognized. Avoid forcing characters to speak or listen to information about facts they already know but which the playwright wants to communicate to the audience. Engage the audience's imagination; implied exposition can be more effective than explicit statements. And distribute exposition throughout the play rather than placing it in large, indigestible chunks.

How can I hide exposition?   Characters should have strong motivation to speak lines containing exposition, so make sure a character delivering exposition has an obvious reason for doing so. Hide exposition materials by placing them in the middle of a speech or sentence, which is the least dominant location; avoid putting them in the beginning or at the end, which are most dominant. And exposition is less noticeable if you give only small bits at a time.

How can I use exposition to propel the action forward?. Henrik Ibsen's *Ghosts* shows that exposition can be more than a mere recitation of past events. Instead of using one large, heavy-handed glob of exposition, as in *A Doll's House*, in *Ghosts* he subtly uses bits of exposition to disclose the past and to motivate the characters; each new discovery of the past changes the characters, moving the play forward.

Should I use a narrator for exposition?. Once popular in classic plays as an introductory device, the narrator is out of fashion in modern theatre. Too often the narrator is simply an all-too-easy way for the playwright to communicate information to the audience, resulting in a play that tells rather than shows. Notable exceptions come to mind, such as Tom in *The Glass Menagerie* and the Stage Manager in *Our Town*, but one easily imagines that hundreds of plays have disappeared or were never produced because the narrator was an intrusive device.

Foreshadowing

"Something wicked this way comes," say the witches in *Macbeth*, illustrating foreshadowing that focuses audience attention on coming events. Foreshadowing is a classic storyteller's device that creates suspense by warning the audience to expect certain events such as a conflict, crisis, complication, entrance of a major character, or an emergency. It also warns of more general effects and signals the play's basic intellectual thrust, as in the first scene of *Macbeth*, where the witches' chant, "Fair is foul, and foul is fair," foreshadows a world that will turn upside down.

Foreshadowing also helps you write. Each piece of foreshadowing is, in effect, a promise you make to yourself to develop plot, focusing your attention on maintaining action. You can test this idea by planning to include, say, three pieces of foreshadowing in the first several pages of your play, and then designing when and how that foreshadowing will take root and grow during the play.

Do I use foreshadowing only in the opening of my play?. No. It can be effective throughout the play, often preparing for a major character's entrance. One does not expect to find it after the climax when action is completed.

Can I write a play without foreshadowing?   Probably, but you'll find it so helpful that you'll want to use it, remembering that, like exposition, foreshadowing is best when subtle. The thunderstorm effect, for example, has become such a cliché in drawing-room melodramas that a modern audience may find it comic instead of ominous.

Plant

A companion to foreshadowing, a plant refers to a physical object that will be important later. If a letter, gun, or the like is significant in the last scene, you can have a character find it by accident at that useful moment, but the convenient coincidence sharply strains credibility. Alternatively, you can *plant* the item by having a character discover it in an early scene, make an idle reference to it, and return it to its location. For example, a character may be looking in drawers for a stamp, happen across the important letter, wonder casually about it, put it back in the drawer, find the stamp, and continue. That plants the letter; its later use will not be a contrived coincidence. Anton Chekhov's advice about plants bears repeating here: "If a gun is hanging on the wall in the first act, it must fire in the last."

General Mood Setting

Beginning playwrights often write a lengthy introduction designed to set the play's mood and environment. Cut those pages ruthlessly. Mood setting seldom is essential and frequently stops the action. If you are genuinely convinced you need to set a mood, make the passages as brief as possible.

Plays should have a basic mood, but you don't have to devote pages to establishing the mood in the introduction. Instead of working to establish a mood, focus your attention on getting to the play's action as soon as you can. Most often the action will set the mood more effectively than long introductory passages.

Point of Attack

Imagine that a large boulder drops into a calm pond, changing the equilibrium and making a series of active waves that, in turn, create more waves. That boulder is like a play's point of attack, destroying the existing balance and causing actions that continue throughout the rest of the play.

Importance of the point of attack.   Arguably the single most important aspect of plot because it begins the play's action, stimulates the protagonist to drive for a goal, and introduces the play's major dramatic question, the point of attack shifts the play from neutral to forward gear. All preceding material is simply introduction and preparation. The point of attack introduces the play's rising action.

For example, in *Hamlet* the point of attack is the Ghost's demand for revenge, which forces Hamlet to take a series of actions that change the balance in the play. In *Oedipus the King,* the point of attack occurs when Creon returns from the oracle with the news that Thebes's plague will end when the murderer of the previous king is identified and punished, and Oedipus immediately promises to accomplish those tasks. In *A Doll's House,* the blackmailer Krogstad introduces the point of attack when he demands that Nora convince her husband to hire him or he will reveal her crime of forgery. In Danai Gurira's *Eclipsed,* the point of attack occurs when The Girl emerges from her hiding place, thus raising the question of what the other wives will do with this vulnerable child. Even Ionesco's "anti-play" *The Bald Soprano,* which in many ways turns traditional dramaturgy upside down, begins with a point of attack when the Martins arrive unexpectedly to spend the evening with the Smiths.

Notice that in each of these cases the point of attack is triggered by an inciting incident in which someone or some event from outside enters the play and disturbs the balance. The point of attack doesn't just happen; it is a response to a disrupting stimulus.

How long is the point of attack?   Think of sustaining the point of attack so it has adequate intensity to change the course of the play, influence the characters, and communicate to the audience. A point of attack can be sustained and clarified when the protagonist questions the necessity of action, resists taking action, or (as in the case of Oedipus) describes his or her intended plan. As a general rule the point of attack may last one or several pages; a single speech is usually not sufficient.

How do I decide where to place the point of attack?   A relatively early point of attack makes your play's beginning more interesting and compelling. "Relatively early" cannot be defined precisely, but a delayed point of attack means the introduction will be filled with exposition, foreshadowing, general mood setting, and the like, which seldom are compelling. The early point of attack in plays as diverse as *Hamlet, Oedipus, Fool for Love,* and *Godot* enhances their drama, in contrast with the delayed point of attack in *A Doll's House,* which makes introductory materials extremely long and tedious for modern audiences.

Which characters must be present at the point of attack?   The point of attack starts the protagonist into action, striving for his or her goal, which means that character necessarily will be present. Frequently the point of attack is triggered by an inciting incident in the form of a character entering from the outside. In many cases, this intruder becomes an important character as the play develops.

The Protagonist's Goal

In the uneasy balance before the point of attack, the protagonist is static, with no reason to take action. The point of attack gives the protagonist a goal, which provides the action of the rest of the play. For example, the Ghost demands revenge at the point of attack in *Hamlet*. Hamlet, the protagonist, then has a goal: He must first find if the Ghost's story is true, then avenge his father's death. The rest of the play is based on Hamlet's actions to achieve his goal. In *Oedipus the King*, the title character clearly states his goal: he will identify the murderer even if the culprit is in his own family (!), and he will punish the perpetrator by execution or exile.

Major Dramatic Question (MDQ)

Elements of plot combine to create the play's action and content. A play's MDQ is a central force that unifies all action and refers to the basic reason you write the play. The MDQ of *A Streetcar Named Desire*, for example, can be simply stated: Can Blanche find the safe haven she must have, at whatever cost to others, if she is to survive? All parts of the play—plot, characterization, meaning—are related to that one issue. The play's action shows Blanche continually working to achieve her goal and, in the process, endangering her sister's marriage.

Most often implied, not directly stated, the MDQ is posed at the point of attack and directly relates to the protagonist's goal and the play's action and intellectual content. The MDQ is answered at the climax, ending the action. For *Streetcar*, the answer is no. Blanche is an intruder whose self-interests will damage the Stanley–Stella marriage, and she cannot find the protection she so desperately needs.

The MDQ provides suspense. The suspense formula is hint—wait—fulfill. The MDQ sets the hint: will the central character achieve her or his goal, and what will happen as a result? This question pulls the audience into the play and, hopefully, sustains their interest as the story develops. The fulfillment of their hopes and fears in the play's conclusion must satisfactorily reward their commitment to the play.

The establishing event, point of attack, and protagonist's goal are linked to the MDQ. *Romeo and Juliet* shows the interrelationship of these aspects of a play. The establishing event, before the play begins, involves the bitter feud between the Capulets and the Montagues. The point of attack occurs when Romeo Montague and Juliet Capulet fall in love. The protagonist's goal—Romeo wants to marry Juliet—is to find love and happiness through marriage. Obstacles to that goal are vividly clear: the deep-seated active hatred between their families. The play's MDQ thus can be stated: Will the powerful love that Romeo and Juliet share be strong enough to overcome their families' deadly animosities? The play's action involves their increasingly desperate attempts to overcome the families' obstacles and complications. The answer to the MDQ—No, love does not conquer all—is clear in the play's climax.

Do I have to know my play's MDQ before I begin to write? Knowing the play's MDQ is a practical approach for writers who work best when they have a complete scenario of the play, giving them a plan so they know precisely where they are going. Others find that too much planning can inhibit the creative process or result in a play that is self-consciously direct. Experience will help you decide what system best fits your working process. Whichever approach you use to write, however, knowledge of your play's MDQ will be important after you've completed the first draft and begin examining your play for revisions.

How do I know if I have a valid MDQ? An effective MDQ combines the present with a drive to a future and links the inciting incident, point of attack, protagonist's goal, obstacles to that goal, and climax. If you find these elements do not have direct causal relationships, you'll want to examine each carefully, looking for possible revisions that will unify your script.

Putting Together the Play's Beginning

To summarize, the traditional structure of a play's beginning includes the following elements: establishing event, state of equilibrium (frequently communicating exposition and foreshadowing), point of attack, protagonist's goal, and major dramatic question. Notice that the most efficient beginnings take place in compressed time. A 10-minute play will best move from beginning to middle by the end of the first page or certainly the second. In a full-length, as previously stated, the play's beginning will best wrap up no later than page 15.

Any number of plays modify this traditional approach to beginnings. For instance, see the analysis of Doug Wright's *I Am My Own Wife* at the end of this chapter for an example of the beginning of a tradition-modifying play. Some plays do away altogether with a clear point of attack, but almost all plays create some sense of foreshadowing in their opening minutes. Lynn Nottage's Pulitzer Prize winning drama *Sweat*, for instance, has no inciting incident or point of attack. However, its first scene makes it clear that a serious crime has been committed for which two men have spent eight years in prison. The rest of the play goes back in time and chronicles the building tensions that eventually result in that crime. That first scene, less than 10 minutes long, establishes a strong MDQ: What did Chris and Jason do to merit eight years in prison, to whom did they do it, and why? These questions are fully answered by the play's violent climax.

Part Two: Middle—The Play's Struggles and Action

A play is a piece of literature about a section of life written in such a way that it will go over the footlights, in such a way that what it has to say it can say in the theatre. That is the sole test. If it can do this it is a play, good or bad. It is a play insofar as the idea, the content, of it is expressed in theatre terms—the space relationships, the oral

*values, the personal medium of the actors, and so on—as
distinguished from the terms of literature.*

— Stark Young

The middle is the longest and most important part of the play. It begins immediately after the point of attack, advances through complications and reversals, and continually builds tensions with forward movement until the height of the tension, or the climax. Part Two is called "rising action," a good description of the desired effect.

Complications, Discoveries, Reversals, Obstacles

Complications, discoveries, reversals, and obstacles have distinctive qualities, but their similarities are more important than their differences. Here we group them all under the term "complications." They are the spark plugs that drive your play's motor by changing the course of its action and provoking the characters to respond and change. For instance, as we noted earlier, the point of attack is the play's first complication, starting the series of dramatic events.

Complications create your play's dramatic tensions by preventing the protagonist from achieving his or her goal. Without them, the protagonist would achieve the goal quickly, easily, and—unfortunately for the play— without conflict and therefore without dramatic values. For example, consider a love story without complications: John proposes to Sally; she says yes; both sets of parents agree; they marry and live happily ever after. End of play. Bland, isn't it? We see only one aspect of the characters because they face no challenges and have no obstacles to overcome; we know little about their love's nature or size because it is not tested; we discover nothing about the writer's personal attitude about love because no thought is developed; and the plot cannot be sustained because nothing happens.

Instead of that tepid and instantly forgettable love story, think of those you've seen or read such as *Midsummer Night's Dream, Camelot, West Side Story, Betrayal*, and *Fool for Love*. Whatever your favorite love story, chances are it attracts you because of the characters' responses to obstacles and complications that impede their love. Those reactions show the depth of their feeling.

"But," "Whoops!" and "Uh-oh."   One way to understand the complication is to think of its effects and how it interrupts, cancels, or changes the characters' plans. We can use lighthearted words to show the complication at work. For example, you may find that creating complications is easier if you use the word *whoops!* as in the example below:

John talks Sally into eloping, when—*whoops!*—her mother catches them as they're at the door. What will they do next?

Or you may prefer to think of a complication as a *but* factor:

> John wants Sally and they begin plans to marry, *but* her father says
> no. That changes the course of the action. Now what will John do?

Alternatively, perhaps it will help if you think of a complication as an *uh-oh* event:

> John and Sally are at their wedding rehearsal when—*uh-oh!*—a woman
> enters, claiming to be John's wife. Now what? How do the characters
> react to this problem?

Note that complications force the characters to react, making them show
other aspects of their personalities and becoming more dimensional.

Typical complications affect the protagonist more than other characters. Such complications fall into categories such as:

- Obstacles posed by antagonists who oppose the protagonist
- The protagonist's personal qualities such as shyness, fear, uncertainty, or alcoholism
- Discoveries about self, others, or significant events such as murder or treachery
- Supernatural or psychic forces influencing the protagonist's physical or spiritual well-being
- Misunderstandings
- Mistaken identities
- Physical hurdles or barriers that the protagonist must overcome

These complications are new problems the protagonist must attempt to
solve to achieve his or her goal.

How many complications should my play have?   Your play has at least
one complication—the point of attack—or else there'd be no action. A one-
act play or short monodrama necessarily has fewer complications than a
full-length, and it is difficult to imagine a successful three-act play without a
number of major complications per act. There is no minimum or maximum
number of complications for a play, but we can suggest that you might want
to work on the premise that you'll have at least one major complication
every five to ten minutes of playing time. Complications can occur almost
every minute, illustrated by movies like *Raiders of the Lost Ark*, plays like
Noises Off, and musicals like *A Funny Thing Happened on the Way to the Forum*.

Entrances Begin Complications

A major character's entrance is a stimulus to the others onstage. An
entrance starts a complication that creates a new direction in the play's
action. It follows that entrances should have sufficient strength to cause
new relationships.

Directors urge playwrights to remember the craft of "building entrances." Playwrights use foreshadowing to prepare the entrance—onstage characters speak anxiously about their concern when the character will arrive—then give the entering person dynamic, elongated action that directly affects the others.

Awareness of stage technique makes you write entrance lines that are long enough and strong enough to bring the character from the door into the room. A short word or two not only fails to sustain the action but also leaves the character standing helplessly at the entrance, forcing the director to move him or her into the room without motivation.

You've seen effective entrances in musical comedies such as *Hello, Dolly!* and *Mame*, when all characters focus on the sweeping entrance of the star, who often comes down a long staircase while singing and dancing. That same technique is applicable, although used more subtly, in dramas.

For example, note the power of the title character's entrance in Molière's *Tartuffe* (as translated by John Wood). Molière famously delayed Tartuffe's entrance until early in the third act of his five-act comedy, but almost every speech prior to that point focuses on this religious hypocrite and his grip on Orgon and his household. Immediately prior to Tartuffe's entrance, the servant Dorine tells Orgon's inflammable son Damis that she thinks Tartuffe has a letch for Orgon's wife, Elmire. Saying Tartuffe has been at prayer but is expected to come down presently, Dorine shoos Damis away so he will not cause a scene, and as he exits, Tartuffe enters. As soon as he spots Dorine, he calls off stage to his servant:

TARTUFFE: Laurent, put away my hair shirt and my scourge and continue to pray Heaven to send you grace. If anyone asks for me I'll be with the prisoners distributing alms.

DORINE: The impudent hypocrite!

TARTUFFE: What do you want?

DORINE: I'm to tell you . . .

TARTUFFE: For Heaven's sake! Before you speak, I pray you take this handkerchief. (*Takes handkerchief from his pocket.*)

DORINE: Whatever do you mean?

TARTUFFE: Cover your bosom. I can't bear to see it. Such pernicious sights give rise to sinful thoughts.

DORINE: You're mighty susceptible to temptation then! The flesh must make a great impression on you! I really don't know why you should get so excited. I can't say that I'm so easily roused. I could see you naked from head to foot and your whole carcass wouldn't tempt me in the least.

TARTUFFE: Pray, speak a little more modestly or I shall have to leave the room.

DORINE: No. No. *I'm* leaving *you*. All I have to say is that the mistress is coming down and would like a word with you.

TARTUFFE: Ah! Most willingly.

DORINE: (*Aside.*) That changes his tune. Upon my word I'm convinced there is something in what I said.

Note the playwright's skill in giving Tartuffe a dynamic entrance. Not only has the audience heard all kinds of things about this character, but Dorine's lines prepare for his immediate entrance, and his obvious parading of his good deeds and high morals, punctuated by Dorine's comments, heighten the impact of his entrance, fully satisfy audience expectations, and set up the next scene in which he will make a pass at Elmire.

Effective Entrances Are Sustained

Note that an entrance means more than the moment the character enters. The arrival of a new person begins a different series of reactions, which continue for a substantial length of time.

Exits Create Complications

Exits, like entrances, change the dynamics of the situation and characters. An exit usually ends one complication and begins another. Like entrances, exits need to be sustained so they will have sufficient strength, involving both the exiting character and those remaining onstage.

Playwrights with a lively sense of theatre know there is a stage technique for exits, which means giving the exiting character enough lines to move physically from, say, the center of the room to the door. To help the character get to the door, the motivation to exit is begun some speeches earlier. After the character's exit, the playwright then shows the new situation for those remaining.

For example, note the well-crafted exit of Nora at the end of *The Doll's House*. She and Torvald Helmer, her husband, have had a long discussion involving his betrayal of her and her realization of the flimsy structure of their relationship. She has declared her intention to leave him and their children, and two minutes before she will walk out, she has gone to fetch her outside clothes and a small bag from the next room. She puts on her cloak, returns Torvald's wedding ring to him and receives hers from him, and warns him not to send her letters or money—

NORA: I take nothing from strangers.
HELMER: Nora—can I never be more than a stranger to you?
NORA: (*Taking her traveling bag.*) Oh, Torvald, then the miracle of miracles would have to happen—
HELMER: What is the miracle of miracles?
NORA: Both of us would have to change so that—Oh, Torvald, I no longer believe in miracles.
HELMER: But *I* will believe. Tell me! We must so change that—?
NORA: That communion between us shall be a marriage. Good-bye. (*She goes out by the hall door.*)
HELMER: (*Sinks into a chair by the door with his face in his hands.*) Nora! Nora! (*He looks round and rises.*) Empty. She is gone. (*A hope springs up in him.*)

Ah! The miracle of miracles—?! (*From below is heard the reverberation of a heavy door closing.*)
THE END

Note the requirements for an effective exit. Repeatedly before her exit Nora shows her motivation. Talking while she makes preparations to leave—getting dressed for outdoors, placing the house keys on the table, picking up her bag—permits her to move toward her exit efficiently but unhurriedly. Since Ibsen wanted to end his play with a sense of finality, there are no extended speeches after Nora's exit, but the way she cuts off all future contacts, their brief discussion of the "miracle of miracles," Helmer's expression of false hope in his last line, punctuated by "the door slam heard 'round the world"—all of these clearly depict Helmer's new reality which Nora leaves in her wake.

Discoveries Instead of Entrances and Exits

Translate "entrances and exits" to "discoveries" to create different forms of complications that create action without characters entering or leaving the room. The discoveries can be internal, like Hamlet gaining new personal insight, or they may take the form of one character discovering a fact about someone else; in either case they begin a new course of action. Often the discovery takes place during a conflict, as in Edward Albee's *Who's Afraid of Virginia Woolf?* which is constructed of continual new complications through arguments.

Acts End with Suspense

Crafting the ending of each act in a full-length play requires you to think of your objectives. Usually you want to complete one major action to give the act a feeling of completion. You also consider creating a hook, something that will make the audience want to return after intermission. Usually this involves a form of suspense, perhaps beginning an interesting action that is not completed when the act ends.

Oscar Wilde creates suspense by using ongoing action at the end of the first act of his elegant comedy, *The Importance of Being Earnest*. Jack, you'll recall, uses the name Ernest in town and Jack in the country, which intrigues his friend, Algernon, who wants to find out just what Jack-Ernest is doing. Algernon, in turn, has invented an imaginary person called Bunbury whom he uses as an excuse to get out of other obligations. As Act One ends, Jack gives Gwendolen his address. Algernon smiles to himself and writes the address on his shirt cuff. In a moment Gwendolen exits. Algernon laughs.

JACK: What on earth are you so amused at?
ALGERNON: Oh, I'm a little anxious about poor Bunbury, that's all.
JACK: If you don't take care, your friend Bunbury will get you into a serious scrape some day.

ALGERNON: I love scrapes. They are the only things that are never serious.
JACK: Oh, that's nonsense, Algy. You never talk anything but nonsense.
ALGERNON: Nobody ever does. (*Jack looks indignantly at him, and leaves the room. ALGERNON lights a cigarette, reads his shirt-cuff and smiles.*)
CURTAIN. END OF ACT ONE.

Just what is Algernon planning? What will he do with the address? Why does he smile? Wilde ends Act One by beginning an action that is designed to make the audience want to return for Act Two to find out how that action will conclude. The audience likely has a good idea what Algernon will do, and they look forward to enjoying the delicious fun with him.

Climax

A play's climax is the major turning point in the dramatic series of events. It shows the outcome of complications, completes the action, and answers the MDQ posed at the point of attack. The protagonist's goal is complete, meeting success or failure, and an equilibrium is being restored. Every scene and incident of the play builds to this point. For the audience member, the climax brings a satisfying feeling that all is logically complete. The climax is inherent in the play's beginning; climax and point of attack are like two bookends that are causally related and encompass the play.

The Climax answers the MDQ.   Think of the climax as the answer to the major dramatic question that was asked at the point of attack: "Will Hamlet avenge his father's death?" "What will be the result of Macbeth's quest for power?" "Will Amanda find a way to protect Laura's uncertain future?"

Should I know my play's climax before I begin writing?   Some playwrights say they write better when they don't know where the play will go. These writers start at the beginning without a clear plan and write through the play, finding the climax when they get there. On the other hand, many playwrights believe they cannot write until they know the climax and they won't begin writing the play until they know its destination. Control of the climax—some complete it before beginning other scenes—allows them to construct their plays backward from that point, making certain that all action leads to the climax. Arthur Miller, for example, started *Death of a Salesman* with only one firm idea: Loman was to destroy himself, motivated by his memories. All the rest of the play, Miller says, was determined by that climax.

Part Three: Ending—A Sense of Finality

In the end, your theme is determined by the way you end your story.
Climax and conclusion dictate the overriding thematic statement of

your story. Therefore, be conscious of how you end your story and
what you are saying by utilizing such an ending.

— RICHARD KREVOLIN

Your play ends with the event that concludes the action; the conflict is resolved; the story does not require any further action or explanation. Your goal in Part Three is to complete the play so it concludes rather than just stopping—and, further, so it ends *once*, without false endings. Part Three, the play's falling action or resolution, contains the denouement and restores the play to an equilibrium.

Denouement

The denouement or resolution is the final knitting together of loose ends. If you write a climax that completes the major questions, the denouement can be quite short. For example, there are only nine speeches in the denouement of *Hamlet*. It reestablishes order and balance to the universe of the play as well as clarifying the future of Denmark which, in the absence of the ruling dynasty, will now be a possession of Norway.

Denouements in modern theatre tend to be brief, avoiding the appearance of knitting together the loose ends. While the resolution may be brief, and while it should not look contrived or manipulated, it is nevertheless an important part of the play and usually should not be omitted. Its primary service is depicting the new balance after the play's action. The plot likely began with a balanced situation (the state of equilibrium) that was disturbed by the point of attack. It advanced through chaos as different characters attempted to establish their own preferred kind of balance. Now the climax has determined what that new balance will be, and the audience wants to know the implications of the new situation. The denouement satisfies that desire.

Many of today's playwrights write suggestive endings, challenging the audience to consider possible solutions to the dilemmas the play has presented and giving them a few options to consider. This technique is perhaps best represented by the conclusion of Gurira's *Eclipsed*. At the end of this play about the plight of women during the Liberian Civil War, four "wives" of a rebel commanding officer (CO) must decide what they will do now that peace has broken out. One, who has just had a baby, elects to stay with the CO; Maima who has become a soldier, declares her intention to keep on fighting; a third decides to go to the city with Rita, a businesswoman, in order to pursue her education. But what about the play's focal character, The Girl, a teenager who has some education but has been recruited as a soldier? What will she do? At the final curtain, she stands holding an assault rifle in one hand and a book in the other, undecided whether to turn one way and follow Maima or the other way to go with Rita. Note that, on the one hand, the playwright doesn't resolve her situation, but on the other hand she does give the audience a clear set of choices that lie before her.

Deus ex Machina

Deus ex machina is not properly a part of plot—some would say it is not part of a proper plot—but we discuss it here to help you avoid its dangers. Literally "god from the machine," the term refers to a device found in the climax of some Greek tragedies when a cranelike machine lowered a god down to the stage. In order to resolve the plot, the playwright brought on a god to solve the hopeless situation.

In modern plays *deus ex machina* refers to any character or action artificially imposed into the play to bring it to a conclusion. It is almost always a mark of poor writing. Avoid the device by maintaining strict quality control over causal relationships, plot construction, and character motivations.

The O. Henry Ending

The short story writer O. Henry (pen name of William Sydney Porter) was best known for sentimental stories with surprise twist endings, exemplified by "The Gift of the Magi," which deals with a poverty-stricken couple, each determined to buy the other a Christmas present. They have no money, only the husband's gold watch and the wife's luxuriously long hair. It ends with a typical surprise: The husband sells his watch to buy her a set of combs for her beautiful hair; she sells her hair to buy him a watch fob.

The best advice to a playwright planning a twist ending is simple: Don't. The device is O. Henry's trademark, and imitations usually lack his individualistic style as well as his talent for setting up his so called "trick" endings. If the trick succeeds at all, it works only with quite short pieces. Finally, such gimmick endings are implausible and tend to insult the audience, which won't appreciate being the butt of the writer's joke. Avoid O. Henry endings if you want your plays to be produced.

Playwright's Curtain Speech

Some playwrights believe they must write a final speech that sums up the play's meaning. Avoid the temptation. Or write it if you must, but throw it away afterward. Instead, make certain that the play's action expresses its meaning. If it does, no curtain speech is necessary; if it doesn't, no curtain speech will correct the problem.

A Twenty-First-Century Plot Sample

As repeated several times throughout this chapter, while particular elements of traditional plot structures have long histories and have shaped hundreds of memorable, successful plays, they have frequently been challenged, reinterpreted, or outright rejected by many playwrights and producers, especially in the late twentieth and twenty-first centuries. The result has created an exciting but sometimes bewildering array of approaches to structuring plays. It's worth taking a little time to look at a twenty-first-century play to see how these elements might be used, laid aside, and reinterpreted. Let's look at Doug Wright's Pulitzer and Tony prize-winning play *I Am My Own Wife* as one sample of such a play.

Several aspects of *I Am My Own Wife* immediately mark it as innovative. On the one hand, it is a bio-drama that depicts the life of Charlotte von Mahlsdorf who was born Lothar Berfelde and lived out her life in drag in Berlin under first the Nazis and then the Communists. On the other hand, as the subtitle of the printed version suggests, this set of "Studies for a Play About the Life of Charlotte von Mahlsdorf" is also about the process of researching to write the play. Indeed, the author himself is a major character in the play. In another departure from recent playwriting, the play includes, in addition to Charlotte and Doug, 33 other speaking characters. And, in yet another major difference from most plays, all of those characters are to be played by a single male actor wearing a black dress. With *I Am My Own Wife* we have clearly entered a nontraditional kind of drama.

And yet, many of the elements discussed in this chapter help form this play's plot, although some of them, like the actor who performs it, may appear in altered garb.

The Beginning

In place of an *initial balance*, the first scene of the play immediately thrusts us into the future (or is it the past?) with Charlotte demonstrating one of the antique phonographs in her museum. In the next scene, a letter from Doug's reporter friend John Marks creates the inciting incident. As it turns out, John is in Berlin covering the fall of the Berlin Wall (the play's *establishing event*?), and his letter tells Doug about Charlotte, "the most singular, eccentric individual the Cold War ever birthed." This letter turns out to be the *inciting incident*, because Doug immediately flies to Berlin and, in the next scene, writes to Charlotte to get permission to interview her for a play. This letter, and Charlotte's letter of acceptance, make up the *point of attack* and reveal that, although the play focuses on Charlotte, structurally Doug is the *protagonist* with the *goal* of writing a play about Charlotte. The unspoken *MDQ* is: Will he bring the play to conclusion? Of course, the suspense that attaches to most MDQs is undercut because the very play that we are watching is, presumably, the one he wants to write. So there we have an almost-complete but somewhat modified beginning with an establishing event, a state of equilibrium consisting of a scene that introduces Charlotte, and an inciting event leading to a point of attack that identifies the central character, poses his goal, and suggests an MDQ.

The Middle

The play intertwines two *substories*. One of these, of course, is Charlotte's biography, and the other is Doug's work interacting with her and John as he pursues his goal of gathering material for his play. Both stories are full of *obstacles, discoveries,* and *complications*. In Act I, for instance, the boy Lothar Berfelde discovers that his aunt Luise is a transvestite who lives as a man and "Charlotte" is born as a result. She faces the obstacle of an abusive father and murders him. And then she is forced by the East German Stasi to become an informer. For his part, Doug not only discovers details about Charlotte but also must cope with the obstacle of his poor German language skills. When he runs out of money (a complication), he has to sell his car. And then, right at the end of Act I, news breaks out that Charlotte was a Stasi informer in the '70s, and her reputation as a generous and courageous homosexual takes a severe blow. This turns out not only to be a major complication but also to create the kind of *end-of-act suspense* that will draw the audience back for Act II.

Act II, then, details some of Charlotte's dealings with the Stasi, including the betrayal of a homosexual business partner of hers who ends up dying in prison as a result. The issue of Charlotte's double dealings becomes a major point of *conflict* between Doug and John, with Doug being somewhat understanding of Charlotte's situation during the East German regime and John insisting that such a double agent should not be memorialized with a play. As the scandal around Charlotte escalates, Doug faces *inner conflict* as he wonders if he should just give up the project, and if he does so, what he will do with all of his research. The next to last scene of the play brings issues to a *climax*; Charlotte, who has moved to Sweden in an attempt to escape her critics, returns to Berlin for a visit and dies of a heart attack amongst her beloved antiques. Doug decides to take a cue from Charlotte who always said the nicks and scratches on her antiques were part of their history; he will write his play, preserving both the good and the bad aspects of Charlotte's character. Clearly there are plenty of complications in these two acts along with conflicts and suspense, and they all lead to a somewhat underplayed climax.

The Ending

In the final scene, Doug describes a picture of young Lothar at a zoo sitting between two lion cubs, either one of which is large enough to attack and kill him, and we hear a bit of a recording of Doug's first interview with Charlotte. While not really a *denouement* that depicts a new balance, this scene provides a kind of nostalgic emotional punctuation to the play, somewhat in the nature of a musical coda on a long symphonic work. With the realistic and yet symbolic picture of the little boy and the two lions, this scene also focuses on aspects of the play's thematic core—the twin poles of Charlotte's counter-culture identity and the compromises she had to make to survive.

EXERCISES USING OTHER PLAYS

1. Teaching others about plot can enhance your own understanding and comprehension. Ask a friend or relative to be your student. First, assign him or her to read a play in which plot elements are clear. Then go through the play identifying and explaining the following terms:

   - Plot
   - Present tense versus past tense; sense of future
   - Establishing event
   - Exposition
   - Foreshadowing
   - Setting a mood
   - State of equilibrium
   - Point of attack
   - Protagonist's goal
   - Protagonist's plan
   - Major dramatic question
   - Complications
   - Climax
   - Deus ex machina
   - Dénouement
   - Playwright's curtain speech

2. Work with a playwright colleague to define the above terms and find them in a play such as *Hamlet*, *Macbeth*, or any other of your choosing.

EXERCISES FOR THE PLAY YOU ARE WRITING

Answers to these exercises should be entered in your writer's journal.

1. Describe the establishing event that sparks your play. When did it happen? How will that incident influence the protagonist? Who was involved in the establishing event?

2. How will the protagonist discover the importance of the establishing event? What is his or her response?

3. Decide to use foreshadowing in your play's beginning. Write several instances of foreshadowing.

4. Write a brief narrative that describes the exposition the audience must know. Decide the barest essentials you'll use in the play's beginning. Plan when you'll use the rest of the exposition later in the play.

5. Outline your play's point of attack. How does it link with the establishing event? What characters are present? Identify the cause of the point of attack, the inciting incident. Write as much of the point of attack as you can, using dialogue, and action.

6. Describe the protagonist's goal. What motivates him or her to achieve that goal? What is the protagonist's emotional involvement in the goal? What is the character's plan?

7. What stops the protagonist from achieving the goal? Who opposes him or her? Why? List a number of complications and obstacles. What are the protagonist's emotional reactions to each obstacle?

8. Put the obstacles in the order they'll occur during the play.

9. Describe the climax of the play you are going to write. Does the protagonist achieve his or her goal? Does the play end "upbeat" or "down?" Be detailed.

10. Show the interrelationship of your play's establishing event, point of attack, protagonist's goal, major dramatic question, and climax. You may wish to create a diagram to show how these fit together.

A good story is obviously a difficult thing to invent, but its difficulty is a poor reason for despising it. It should have coherence and sufficient probability for the needs of the theme; it should be of a nature to display the development of character . . . and it should have completeness, so that when it is finally unfolded no more questions can be asked about the persons who take part in it. It should have, like Aristotle's tragedy, a beginning, a middle, and an end.

— W. Somerset Maugham

ADDITIONAL READING ON THE TOPICS OF THIS CHAPTER

Ball, David. *Backwards and Forwards: A Technical Manual for Reading Plays.* Southern Illinois University Press, 1983. A play analysis system for traditionally structured plays.

Castagno, Paul C. *New Playwriting Strategies: Language and Media in the 21st Century.* 2nd ed. Routledge, 2011. Ch. 9 "Units and Building Blocks" and ch. 10 "Scenes, Acts, and Revisions." Approaches to plotting in dialogic plays.

Smiley, Sam with Norman A. Bert. *Playwriting: The Structure of Action.* 2nd ed. Yale University Press, 2005. Ch. 4 "Plot" and ch. 5 "Story." A complete and in-depth treatment of plot and story elements in the Aristotelian tradition.

6

Creating Characters
People in Action to Achieve Their Goals

> *I deliberately look for colorful people. They're very right for theatre. Theatre has to be theatrical. If you can get color into the accountant, you've got something. Write the whole thing first and then say he's an accountant. That's a very wacky accountant, but so what? Theatricality feeds and challenges the actor, the director, and the designers.*
>
> — LANFORD WILSON

If plot is the skeleton and muscles that hold the play together, then characters are the soul, spirit, flesh, and blood that drive your play. Characters have basic superobjectives that create the conflict and twists and turns that form plot, and plot provides complications and stimuli that force characters to react and change. Neither plot nor character exists independently of the other; each contributes to the development of its partner. Being a playwright means developing character and plot equally so each enriches the other.

Whether you believe plot or character is more important in writing for the theatre, one premise is inescapable: *Plays that involve interesting characters in conflict are more effective than plays that do not.* As August Strindberg said, playwriting requires "seeking out the points where the great battles take place." Dramatic intensity, comic or tragic, is a product of characters willing to battle to achieve something highly important to them that gives them a personal involvement in the struggle and outcome. "Great battles" make characters dimensional and interesting. The battles also make them easier, even fun, to write because their intense concerns are so active that they often dictate what they want to do, sometimes making the playwright think the characters are writing the play themselves.

Exercises you completed in previous chapters have started your identification of characters you'd like to create, and your writer's notebook should be full of ideas and materials you can use to develop your play. Here we look at using those notes to create theatrical characters.

Writing Effective Characters

Being a playwright requires constructing theatrical characters who give actors artistic challenges with playable emotions and actions to help them bring characters to life as you intend. Effective characters sustain interest in your play by communicating to the audience so they can understand and appreciate your play's action and theme. Dynamic, colorful, contrasting, active, and clear characters serve your needs. Such characters will also attract the attention of producers and directors and make them want to present your play.

Actions Show Characters

Although other clues are helpful (like other characters' descriptions or stage directions), producers, directors, and actors look for characters who are shown primarily by actions; therefore you write dimensional characters who are a direct result of the incidents that stimulate them to act. Think of your characters—especially the major ones—progressing, evolving, unfolding, in motivated steps. You want to think in present tense, building characters who are thinking "I am doing" instead of "I did," and are aware of their future, thinking "I want to achieve" an important goal.

Clues to Character

Directors, actors, and audiences learn about characters through certain clues you give them. Among the primary clues are the following:
- What the character does; action
- What the character will not do; action through inaction
- What the character says
- What the character does not say; communication through silence
- The character's emotional range
- What the character wants; goals
- Why the character acts, speaks, or seeks a goal; motivation
- How the character responds to stimuli
- Characters' self-descriptions

- Descriptions by others
- Characters' names
- Stage directions, descriptions
- The play's environment

Throughout this chapter we'll examine how you use these clues.

Forces That Shape Us.
Forces That Shape Our Characters

Characters are entities, constructed by playwrights, which carry out the actions of plays. Characters look like real people, but characters are not real people. What makes you and me what we are? Why do we believe what we believe, want what we want, and do what we do? Most people would answer that our genetic makeup and our experiences—nature and nurture, heredity and environment—make us what and who we are. What makes a character what he or she is? Very simply, the play-wright's decisions, be those decisions conscious or intuitive. We are the creatures of our heredity and environments; characters are the creatures of their playwrights. Of course, many characters *appear* to have been shaped by their genetics and experiences, but those shaping forces are supplied to help audiences accept them as real people and understand their motivations and actions. In this section, we will investigate some of the forces that you can use to shape your characters.

External Traits of Characters

External traits—what the audience sees and hears about your characters—these things both shape the characters and also reveal them.

Age. How old are your characters? Age influences behavior—a teenager reacts to certain stimuli differently from the way an older person does—and therefore you can use it to indicate characters' special qualities, experience, and view of the world. For example, the youth of the central characters in *Heathers, The Musical* creates an explosive, hormone-driven situation while the supposedly mature age of the parents and school authorities in the musical accents their ineptitude and clarifies that they will be of no help in guiding the adolescents through their problems.

Physical characteristics and mannerisms. What physical details do your characters have? Characters may have particular physical conditions or may even pose or posture to indicate certain behavioral mannerisms such as pomposity, vulnerability, or the like. In Lisa Kron's *Well*, for example, Ann's exploitation of her disabilities contrasts sharply with her daughter's intention to be well. Laura's crippled leg in *The Glass Menag-*

erie and Stan's leg injury from an industrial accident in Lynn Nottage's *Sweat* both show deeper details about these characters while also connecting directly with their plays' thematic impacts. Use such mannerisms and physical conditions judiciously to depict character traits.

Vocal mannerisms. How do your characters talk? Some characters may speak hesitantly and others speak quickly and authoritatively. You can describe such mannerisms in stage directions, but dialogue is a more important tool. For example, in *The Caretaker*, Harold Pinter uses dialogue to show a character's internal turmoil: "But . . . but . . . look . . . listen . . . listen here . . . I mean . . . What am I going to do? (*Pause*) What shall I do? (*Pause*) Where am I to go?" And, of course, the entire plot of Shaw's *Pygmalion* turns on Eliza Doolittle's manner of speaking.

Overall appearance. Is each of your characters neat? Messy? Proud or indifferent about appearance? Why? How does that exterior appearance reveal the inner person? Directors, actors, and costume designers will take the playwright's statements, plus the character's clues, to create a special visual quality that depicts the character. You use stage directions to help those artists visualize each character; more importantly, you guide them by the character's behavior and actions.

Environmental Impacts on Characters

As you develop your characters, consider the many environmental forces that have made them what they are.

Time and place. Characters often react to and are part of the time in which the action takes place (the era, the year, the season, the hour of day or night). *Cat on a Hot Tin Roof*, for instance, takes place in the 1950s, not long after World War II, on Big Daddy's birthday which also turns out to be the day that he and his family learn that he's dying of cancer. Each of these time details shapes the behaviors of the characters in this play.

Furthermore, characters are influenced by their locale, such as the visible setting in which the play takes place (a room or bus station, for example), the outside environment (small town, metropolitan area, and so forth), and the particular region (Southern or Western, for example). The brothers and parents on the Southern plantation in Williams's play have completely different expectations and modes of behavior than the brothers and mother in Sam Shepard's *True West* set on the edge of the California desert.

Educational background. The educational level(s) of the characters, as a group or as individuals, contributes to who they are. Are your characters college-trained? Did they fail to graduate from high school? Does that educational background influence how they feel about themselves and what they say and do? The primary characters in Eugene O'Neill's

The Hairy Ape have little or no educational background, a fact that influences their speech and actions; in contrast, characters in Edward Albee's *Who's Afraid of Virginia Woolf?* are well-read, literate college graduates, as shown in their dialogue and actions.

Economic situation, social and political environments.   Wealthy, poor, or middle class, the economic status of the characters can dictate their attitudes and actions. The well-to-do film stars in Neil LaBute's *The Money Shot*, for instance, have far different goals and expectations than the workers in Nottage's *Sweat* who are sinking into poverty as the economy bottoms out. And characters form a particular structure within the play—the pecking order, so to speak—and also may be involved in a larger political issues. In LaBute's play, for instance, the two stars begin the play clearly superior to their companions, and the audience watches with naughty joy as the tables are turned, while the characters in *Sweat* live at the mercy of political and economic forces beyond their control.

Religious backgrounds.   Characters are influenced by an implied or explicit presence or absence of a deity-structured universe and also by their individual religious backgrounds. Classical Greek plays such as Sophocles's *Oedipus Rex* show humans with direct relationships to their gods while the characters in Lucas Hnath's *The Christians* are torn apart in their different perceptions of what God wants from them. And other plays such as Samuel Beckett's *Waiting for Godot* take place in an environment devoid of religious guidance.

Bringing It Together through Biography

One way to explore all these different traits and influences is to write a biography of each of your characters. Some playwrights claim never to begin writing dialogue until they have written pages-long biographies of each of their characters. Some questions that might underlie such biographies include:

> Where was the character born? Who were his/her parents? What were their occupations? What were the character's largest successes in high school? Failures? Who was his/her first love? Why? What did he/she do while in love? How did the character handle the loss of that love? How did he/she react to various rites of passage such as adolescence, first sexual experiences, reaching the age of majority, marriage, first child, divorce, death of a relative, and so forth? What did the character dream of doing with his/her life? How does the character feel now about those dreams?

Writing each character's life story will give you answers to such questions, which in turn will give you new insight into the characters, resulting in richer and more dimensional characterization.

Objectives

Having invented or discovered each of your character's traits, influences, and biography, you will have well-developed, richly endowed characters. Eventually, you will need to bring all of these details into a unity. At that point, if you haven't already considered them, you will want to identify the character's objectives. A character's objectives range from small, moment-to-moment intentions to the major goal that he or she wants to accomplish within the play—what some actors call the *superobjective* and others call the character's *story goal*. Usually, all of a character's small intentions add up to that overreaching superobjective. In a traditionally structured play, the central character's superobjective will likely be revealed in the play's point of attack, but even a minor character will be more effective if the playwright clearly understands what drives him or her. State character objectives by beginning: "The character wants to—." Follow with an active verb, one that clarifies how the character will know whether or not he or she has achieved the goal. For instance, Oedipus wants *to be respected*, but then he already *is* respected, even at the beginning of the play. What drives him throughout is his objective *to find and punish the murderer of Laius, thus purging Thebes of its plague*. Aim to unify each of your characters by identifying each one's superobjective.

Sources for Theatrical Characters

I think it's true of most playwrights that their characters—male and female, young and old—are just aspects of themselves. When I people the stage with all these souls, what I do is split myself up. I implode and all these little fragments tear around inside me like crazy and become the characters.

— Tina Howe

The Writer's Eye

According to playwright Mario Fratti, theatre "is a window open on the lives of our fellow creatures." Being a playwright requires a special desire to open windows that allow you to see the people around you, carefully observing humans in action, noting how they show attitudes and emotions. Look around. The reclusive woman on the corner who is the subject of neighborhood rumors, the recently divorced man with a new flaming red sports car, the latchkey teenager who is known as a troublemaker, the church elder recently convicted of purchasing kiddie porn, the medical doctor who changed careers and now teaches third grade— your writer's eye observes these and other people in your world, and your imagination works to understand them.

With your writer's eye you spy into other humans, gaining insights that lead you to write characters who show their feelings. Some writers say that their eye is disturbingly active even during highly emotional personal experiences such as funerals, marriages, family breakups, and childbirth. One portion of the writer is deeply involved in the situation, but another portion is observing the other participants, recording them for future writing. The spying doesn't always please friends or family members: James Thurber said his wife often came up to him at parties and demanded, "Thurber, stop writing!" A writer's eye notes tensions, emotions, motivations, and concrete actions, not abstract descriptions.

Ideas for characters come from various sources, and perhaps you'll be one of the fortunate playwrights with a large flow of possibilities for plays. If the well appears dry, however, don't despair and—most importantly—don't stop writing. You can stimulate your creative energy by exploring your world for new ideas. We indicate some major sources below.

Yourself

Tina Howe, author of *Painting Churches*, says that a basic source for characters is the playwright's self. Many writers agree. Much of what you write is necessarily autobiographical, and it is wise to allow yourself freedom to let your plays reflect portions of your beliefs, attitudes, ethical and religious standards, memories, dreams fulfilled or lost, family relationships, frustrations, loves, angers, and other aspects of your inner self.

"Every character I imagine is part of me," says playwright Maria Irene Fornes. You don't have to be a murderer to write a character who is a killer, but you do reach into recesses of your inner self to find emotions that might lead to killing someone, and you examine your memories for times that you took violent actions that your imagination enlarges and expands to help you get into the nature of the particular killer you need for your play. As Fornes says about using herself to create characters, "The sadistic captain in *The Conduct of Life* and the victim of that sadistic captain—you can't write them unless you are them. If a character is brutal, it is because I am brutal. I take the blame and the credit. No writer can write a character unless she understands it thoroughly inside herself."

Some playwrights find that their most meaningful events involve their families because such relationships are filled with powerful emotions that deeply influence the writer. Personal familial experience can lead to excellent autobiographical dramas or comedies, evidenced by plays such as Eugene O'Neill's *Long Day's Journey into Night*, Tennessee Williams's *The Glass Menagerie*, and Neil Simon's trilogy, *Brighton Beach Memoirs*, *Biloxi Blues*, and *Broadway Bound*.

Alternatively, you may want to create a less recognizable, indirect reflection of yourself or a metaphor for an important aspect of your life. Playwright David Hwang says, "I'm quite aware of the extent to which my own life is embedded in the things I write. I'd like to think it's not obvious to the casual observer. Essentially, what I do is take the essence of the experience and transmute it into a form where the specifics are different. Take *Dance and the Railroad*. I've never worked on a railroad, but I have understood what it is like to be at war with yourself over your own artistic impulses in the battle between commerce and art." That indirect, metaphorical approach can be highly successful, as indicated by plays such as Arthur Miller's *The Crucible* and *After the Fall*.

You may also disguise autobiographical qualities to the point that not even your closest friends or relatives will recognize your presence in the play. You're the fountainhead of the character's origin, but the play, like a broad river, then takes its own course. Expect the artistic needs of the play to require reshaping or changing events, situations, and characters. Such changes probably will further disguise the actual incidents, but nevertheless the play captures the essences of the experience.

Friends and Relatives

Next to yourself, you are most familiar with friends, relatives, and associates. Your close knowledge of them can help you draw dimensional characters in your play. Study those people you know best, seeking to understand their actions, emotions, motives, beliefs, driving forces, ethical standards, dreams, ambitions, and reasons for behavior. You'll discover aspects of character that can help you write your play.

Imagine, for example, that your play requires a protagonist who is liked and respected by others in the play, and you want the audience to have similar reactions. To help you create that protagonist, select a close friend you and others respect and carefully study his or her character, paying special attention to actions. Select specific instances when your friend took particular actions and then adapt those actions for use by your protagonist. Comparable observed behaviors, positive or negative, can become part of other characters.

You can draw from friends or relatives to find ideas for plays as well as characters. Neil Simon says he wrote a play about his brother Danny. "I saw the story being lived out," Simon says. He suggested that his brother write it himself: "What's going on between you and Roy Gerber? It's a play. Two guys living alone, and the two of you are fighting like husband and wife. You've got to write it as a play." Danny did write about fifteen pages but was unable to see how to complete it, so Neil wrote it: *The Odd Couple*.

The greatest danger in using yourself or a close friend or family member as a model for a character is the inability to distance yourself from your model. Remember at all times that you're not writing a history, you're composing a play. The character must be adapted to the play and fictionalized as necessary to fulfill the play's needs.

News Media Stories

Local, national, and international events provide excellent ideas for plays, and the news media are filled with materials you may shape into a comedy or tragedy. Look for stories that deal with personalities, problems, politics, and the like. News accounts, however, tend to treat stories in an abstract, dispassionate tone, requiring you to invent a more personalized, often smaller scale that involves specific humans. For example, a news story about a famine striking an entire country might become a play if you envision a character attempting to overcome problems delivering food to a small village, perhaps in conflict with an indifferent, greedy bureaucrat who cares more for personal gain than for the starving people. Other stories may be more complete, needing only your imaginative shaping and personal point of view. For instance, news accounts about a date rape or a hate-crime victim may be ready to build into a play because they already have protagonist, antagonist, and plot.

The Imaginative Composite

Theatrical characters most often are composites, one trait from a friend, a second personality quality from a relative, attitudes or experiences from your own past, and so forth. Your imagination blends the pieces into one character, and as Lillian Hellman notes, the character's independence, and the artistic needs of the play will dictate further changes.

> *I don't think characters turn out the way you think they are going to turn out. They don't always go your way. If I wanted to start writing about you, by page ten I probably wouldn't be. I don't think you start with a person. I think you start with the parts of many people. Drama has to do with conflict in people, with denials.*
> — Lillian Hellman

Necessary Characters for Your Play

Identifying the essential people for your play's action is your first priority in planning the play's list of characters. In one of playwriting's paradoxes (and if you're thinking theatre is constructed with paradoxes, I quite agree with you), you think of the characters in two different ways, as independent humans yet also as pawns who serve the play.

Theatrical Characters Have Independent Lives

On one hand, you want to see each character as a unique human with strong emotions, desires, traits, and mannerisms. Creating a dimensional character requires knowledge of his or her background, parents, friends, education, occupation, and dozens of other details. In this sense you want to create characters with independent lives aside from the play.

Theatrical Characters Serve the Play

On the other hand, although each character is independent, each must also serve your play, filling specific functions in the overall scheme of the play. In this sense, each is an important tactical chess piece you use to develop your play's strategy. Think of characters as contributors to the theatre's logic and needs; create characters who will perform the actions that your play's structure and development require. Two major characters that serve your play and provide the central conflict are the protagonist and the antagonist.

The Protagonist

The word protagonist has several sources. *Pro* means for, and *agon* means struggle or act, and therefore a protagonist is a character who struggles for a goal, acting to achieve something. The term also comes to us from the Greek word that means first combatant, an excellent description of your play's major character because the protagonist's struggles are the source of dramatic action.

In effective plays there is often one dominant force: A central character has a deep desire, even a compulsion, to achieve something. The protagonist pursues that superobjective despite all opposition—other characters, interior personal doubts, environmental or hereditary influences, even fate or the gods—until he or she wins or loses.

Drama comes alive when a protagonist with a goal, a combatant eager to win a particular victory, runs up against equally strong opposition. Granted, a play can succeed without a protagonist, but a protagonist can contribute many advantages to your play's conflict, tensions, character interplays, meaning, organization, and plot. Whether exemplary hero or, more typically, a lesser mortal with human weaknesses but still trying to achieve something, a protagonist can keep your play in focus by engaging the audience's interest and emotions, and giving them a connecting point through whose eyes they view the action.

The Protagonist's Contributions to Your Play

The protagonist is your play's central character; his or her active need to achieve a goal can give your play action, life, power, and unity. The protagonist's drive for a goal also helps you organize the play's structure or plot. For example, the plot movements in *The Glass Menagerie* are a direct result of Amanda's overpowering need to give Laura a secure future—in Amanda's terms, that means a husband—and the play's action, characterization, and diction are logical outgrowths of the protagonist's objective.

The Protagonist Awakens Audience Interest and Emotions

As the protagonist propels your play forward, initiating and receiving action, it creates audience interest in the outcome. Because the protagonist has something vitally important at stake and therefore is emotionally involved in the action, he or she awakens the audience's emotional reactions and gives them someone for whom they can care.

The Protagonist Shows the Play's Meaning

The audience perceives your play's thematic core through the protagonist's struggles and actions to achieve his or her goal. For example, through Macbeth's increasingly desperate actions to gain more power, the audience understands the play's basic meaning about power's ability to corrupt. In *Death of a Salesman*, Willy Loman's struggles to make his son love him illustrate the playwright's thematic concept about disasters that occur when moral values are badly warped.

The Protagonist's Goal

The protagonist almost always has a goal, either clearly stated or implied. The goal may be meticulously planned or haphazard, conscious or subconscious. You'll find the protagonist's goal stated explicitly in some plays, such as *Hamlet*, Sam Shepard's *Fool for Love*, and Samuel Beckett's *Waiting for Godot*. The goal is implied by the protagonist's actions in other plays, such as *Macbeth*, Henrik Ibsen's *A Doll's House*, and Arthur Miller's *Death of a Salesman*. Regardless of how explicitly your play states the protagonist's goal, you will do well to know it yourself. Otherwise the character may wander aimlessly, and the play's structure may be haphazard.

Why create a protagonist with a major goal? The protagonist's goal helps you write your play by giving your plot a central struggle. It also is important for actors and directors involved with bringing your play to life.

The Protagonist's Plan

The protagonist's goal produces a master plan of action that begins at your play's point of attack. The plan may be implied through the situation or explicitly stated, such as Hamlet's speech, "The play's the thing wherein I'll catch the conscience of the king." The protagonist may have to devise additional or secondary goals to overcome obstacles, but the master goal always dictates his or her actions and sustains the play's action until the climax.

Using the Protagonist's Goal in Your First Plays

Your writing process will be easier if you continually ask questions such as: "What does my protagonist want? Why? What stops him or her from getting it? How does the protagonist respond to each of those obstacles? What emotions drive him or her to pursue that goal?" Answers will help you shape the play's conflict while also developing the play's characters. Write the goal and plan on a piece of paper, tack it to a bulletin board above your keyboard, and refer to it often as you construct your play.

The Antagonist

Drama thrives on conflict, the arrangement of force versus counterforce, conscious will to achieve a goal against equally determined opposing will, one individual (the protagonist) against at least one and sometimes several adversaries (the antagonist). Hamlet must achieve his goal—to avenge his father—and is opposed by his mother and uncle. Lear has every reason to want to achieve his goal—to keep the trappings but not the responsibilities of being a king—and is thwarted by two of his daughters and their husbands.

Antagonists Contribute to the Play's Action

If there were no force–counterforce, there'd be no conflict. An antagonist helps you sustain your play's structure of action: Each step the protagonist takes to achieve his or her goal is opposed by the antagonist, creating complications that maintain the plot. The antagonist can be a single, powerfully compelling character like Iago or can be a number of characters like those who oppose Cyrano de Bergerac.

Antagonists Must Be Worthy Opponents

We measure our fellow humans by the size of the obstacles they encounter and the manner in which they struggle against adversaries, admiring those who tackle fearsome odds. There's little honor in bashing a weak opponent. For many of us the final outcome is less interesting than the struggle; responses to opponents, win or lose, are fascinating because those struggles give us insight into the person. So, too, your protagonist's character is tested and shown by reactions to the antagonist, such as Proctor's struggles against the forces of blind intolerance in *The Crucible*. A strong antagonist gives you opportunity to develop the protagonist's character and helps you structure and sustain the play's action.

The Antagonist Makes the Characters More Dimensional

The importance of the antagonist as a counterforce is illustrated by Lear, who changes and evokes audience emotional responses only because of the actions of his two daughters: If those counterforces did not exist, Lear would never need to change. With an antagonist, your protagonist has reasons to react, change, and evolve as a result of new stimuli the antagonist provides.

The Antagonist within the Protagonist

Interior doubts.   Hamlet doubts his ability to find a proper course of action; Amanda Wingfield's unreal expectations stop her from finding a path to help Laura; Willy Loman doesn't recognize his values are so wrong; John Proctor is so guilt-burdened over his affair with Abigail that he is ambivalent about taking action to correct moral mistakes in his society; and Charlotte Von Mahlsdorf must compromise her principles if she is to survive. In these sorts of plays, the protagonist must battle a strong inside opposing force, an interior antagonist that both gives the character dimension and contributes tension and conflict to the play.

Exterior representation of inner doubts.   A character battling his or her own self is intriguing, but exterior forces—the antagonist characters—show the interior battle and provide visible and playable conflict. Hamlet, for example, is opposed not only by himself but also by a number of antagonists, most notably Gertrude and Claudius. For Charlotte Von Mahlsdorf, the Stasi trigger and personalize her inner conflicts. By all means, think of your protagonist's interior battles, doubts, and insecurities as you plan your play, but think also of exterior representation of those struggles.

Secondary Characters Serve the Play

It is possible to write an effective two-character one-act or, less frequently, full-length play, focused on protagonist against antagonist, but additional characters can add fire and dimension. A two-hander can grow static, while additional characters add conflict and interest. More important, other characters make your writing process easier by providing necessary stimuli to force protagonist and antagonist into further action.

Characters have independent lives . . .   The paradox we mentioned earlier—characters as individualized people simultaneously being servants of your play—also applies to secondary characters. Like the protagonist and antagonist, they must have independent lives and a significant role to play in the development of both the protagonist and the play's action. In this sense you write characters who are distinct individuals, not types.

. . . but characters also are masks of dramatic action.   On the other hand, secondary characters also serve your play's structure and growth by emphasizing the conflict and adding tension to the situation. Although Richard Schechner refers to directors and actors, his point is equally pertinent for playwrights when he speaks about characters serving the play: "Great errors are made because performers and directors [we would add playwrights] think of characters as people rather than as *dramatis personae:* masks of dramatic action. A role conforms to the logic

of theatre, not the logic of any other life system. To think of a role as a person is like picnicking on a landscape painting." In this sense you write characters who fall into theatrical categories to serve structural needs.

Examples of Secondary Characters "Serving the Play"

What do we mean by characters serving the play? How do you use them? Because the entrance of a new character usually is a complication, you use secondary characters to spark the plot by judiciously planning when they enter the scene, perhaps bringing in a new character when the play begins to drag due to lack of new insights or flagging conflicts, and because they can be drawn to contrast with the major characters, you shape them to point up the special traits of protagonist and antagonist. Use them, too, to add texture, color, differences, and other qualities to enhance your play.

The poker players in *Streetcar* illustrate a playwright's use of secondary characters to make major contributions to the play's primary characters and structure. Although the players are not fully developed and one might argue that they should be eliminated because they are not essential to the play, they are important in a number of ways:

- The game shows Stanley's macho character as he plays poker with "the boys."

- During the game Stanley is crude and authoritative, even dictatorial, giving the playwright another way of showing that Stanley is king of his castle.

- The poker players amplify Stanley's character. If Williams had written the play with only Stanley visible, audiences might conclude that all males in that universe are dictatorial. But putting other males in contrast to Stanley reinforces his particular values and behaviors. The scene shows that Stanley is not like other males in the world of this play.

- The scene allows Williams another opportunity to use different techniques to show aspects of Blanche's character as she displays herself seductively, standing in bra and thin slip with the light behind her, yet carefully making her actions appear accidental. The action shows the character clearly: She uses sex to get attention while pretending to be the quintessential "lady." It reinforces Stanley's complaint that Blanche is pretentious and hypocritical, and it contributes to Stanley's motivation to rape her ("We've had this date with each other from the beginning!" he says, referring to her displays of her body).

- The poker game serves to introduce Mitch and Blanche. Although Williams could have invented another device to put the two together, this approach helps show Mitch's immediate fascination with her: He stays with her instead of returning to the poker game, even after Stanley shouts for him to return.

- The scene serves as a change of pace. Much of the play prior to this scene had been constructed with duets and trios involving Stanley, Stella, and Blanche; the poker game brings other people into the play, making a refreshing change.

A Secondary Character: The Visible Objective

Amanda's objective—a husband for Laura—influences the structure of *The Glass Menagerie*. Williams could have written the play with references to various possible suitors, describing Laura's various encounters with them, but that would have decreased the play's emphasis on present and future. Amanda's objective almost forces the playwright to bring the suitor onstage, leading to the creation of the Gentleman Caller, visibly showing Amanda's objective. So, too, Mitch is a visible objective in *Streetcar*, showing Blanche's need for someone to take care of her. Without Mitch the play would not show the growth of Blanche's hopes and her subsequent despair. Consider developing your play with a character who will turn an abstract objective into a human reality.

A Secondary Character: The Close Friend

In *The Crucible*, Proctor has his wife; in *A Doll's House*, Nora has Mrs. Linden; in *Cyrano de Bergerac*, Cyrano has Le Bret; in *Death of a Salesman*, Willy Loman has Ben; and in *Sweat*, the bartender Stan is everyone's friend. These close friends are *confidant(e)s* with whom other characters can share inner thoughts, plans, or doubts that otherwise would have to be expressed in a soliloquy. If you find that your protagonist needs opportunities to express personal secrets, consider building a close friend into your play.

A Secondary Character: The Foil

We learn more about central characters when we can compare and contrast them with others who are similar in some ways but different in others. These characters who provide these kinds of contrasts are *foils*. For instance, we gain a clearer understanding of Brick in *Cat on a Hot Tin Roof* by seeing him in contrast with his brother Gooper, and we have a stronger picture of Maggie in that play by contrasting her with her sister-in-law Mae.

Other Secondary Characters

There are any number of additional dramatic functions that can be served by secondary characters. Playwrights and theorists have identified many of these: *raisonneurs* (supporters) who express the playwrights' viewpoints; messengers who bring in news from off stage; narrators who give background information; arbiters who settle conflicts. Some forms have their own sets of functions; melodramas, for instance, are populated by heroes, heroines, villains, wise old fathers or mothers, comics, and so on. The list goes on and on.

Two important observations: First, every character in your play should have a specific function. Characters who don't serve a function directly related to the play's action or thematic core should be eliminated.

In this regard, pay particular attention to *utility characters* whose only function is to carry out tasks unrelated to the play's action or theme. Examples include waiters in plays set in restaurants, postal workers who deliver letters, and so on. A specific example is the policeman who arrests Mr. Zero in Elmer Rice's *The Adding Machine*; the policeman is onstage perhaps 30 seconds, never to appear again, and his only function is the arrest. Such characters must be cast and costumed, thus causing additional expense, and the actors in those unrewarding roles must attend almost as many rehearsals as the principals. If you find yourself placing a utility character in your play, you have several options. You might simply eliminate that character and find a different way to accomplish the small task he or she executes. Or you might combine it with other small roles in the play. Or give that character a stake in the play's action. The aforementioned Stan in *Sweat*, for instance, not only tends bar but also serves as a confidant, becomes the play's voice of reason, illustrates by his disability the inhumanity of factory management, and deepens the play's pathos when he is victimized in the play's climax.

Finally, notice that a single character may serve multiple functions in different scenes throughout the play. Characters are not limited to serving a single function alone.

Creating Theatrical Characters

Just before I started working on Hot L Baltimore, *I read Dickens's* Our Mutual Friend. *I had just done* Lemon Sky *and* Serenading Louie, *and they seemed pale and quaint compared to Dickens. I knew I had to goose my work. I knew I had to have characters that were more far-out. Your characters have to have some magic.*

— Lanford Wilson

Wilson took his own advice, finding "magic" not only for characters in *Hot L Baltimore*, but for his many other plays, including *Fifth of July* and *Burn This*, making him an acknowledged master of characterization. If that's the result of "goosing" characters and making them "more far-out," he proves that his advice works.

Effective theatrical characters are vivid, unusual, and different, yet they must also be plausible, possible, and probable within the basic concept of the play. Dimensional characters are like onions, constructed of layers of traits that are slowly disclosed to the audience, with surprises that nonetheless are still an inherent part of the onion's core.

Creating characters for your play is a process similar to the novelist's, with some important differences: Theatrical characters must be playable, which means you write for actors to show thoughts and emotions. And they must have a basic instant clarity so the audience can recognize their driving force.

The Tip of the Iceberg

Dimensional and interesting characters are structured like icebergs: Although only one-tenth shows above the surface, they are supported by a foundation that is nine-tenths of the whole. The better you know your characters, the stronger they will be and the more new ideas you'll find about their personality and actions. You'll discover interesting traits, emotions, and drives by expanding your view past the actual play, paying special attention to aspects that will not show in the play. Construct lengthy notes about the characters' lives before and after their lives onstage (Where were they before they entered? Where will they go when they leave?) and before and after the specific action of the play.

Emotions

Theatre is the art of emotions; emotional action is the play's life force. Emotions give your characters a rich vitality, making the play snap and crackle. Try to give each character a primary energizing emotion—ambition, fear, anger—connected to his or her basic goal. Major characters should also have emotional ranges and motivated changes—such as happiness interrupted by sadness and anger, laughter mixed with tears, and the like—although you may decide that a single emotion is adequate for secondary characters. Blanche, for example, goes through a wide range of emotions; Mitch has only two (love for Blanche, followed by anger that she lied to him); the poker players have one at most.

Unique Fingerprints, Not "Typical"

Just as each human has unique fingerprints and DNA charts, each of your characters has his or her distinctive individuality. Avoid stereotypes or thinking of "typical" characters. Instead create characters who have a variety of qualities that make them unlike any other person.

Start with One Basic Characteristic

To maintain focus and clarity of purpose, try starting your creative process by identifying a single dominant characteristic for each of the people in your play. Although you want dimensional humans with more than one trait, effective characterization starts with making choices, selecting the one major trait or attribute that drives the character. For example, the three fascinating characters in Jean-Paul Sartre's *No Exit* are based on quickly perceived attributes: the coward, the lesbian, and the nymphomaniac.

Starting with single qualities is not as simplistic as it might sound. First, each character's major quality doesn't show up by itself but instead contributes to the whole picture just as various individual colors in a painting will create a totality. Second, your knowledge of dominant qualities will help you keep the characters consistent and dynamic within their basic parameters. Third, clarity of qualities will help directors and actors bring your play to life as you intend, but if the characters are murky, the actors may perform their roles differently from the way you wish.

After you've clearly identified each character's distinctive attribute, build on that foundation by adding other personality elements. For example, the coward wants to be alone and pretends to be an intellectual, the lesbian enjoys being cruel and is more intelligent and manipulative than the others, the nymphomaniac desperately needs attention and acts various roles to please others, and so forth.

Heightened Life

Playwrights tend to think of their characters as real people; however, this does not mean that theatrical characters *are* real people. Your characters are instead a form of heightened reality, selectively enlarged to show their special traits and desires. Drama is not life but an artistically selected representation of life; equally, theatrical characters are heightened representations of real people. In life, an individual's crisis may evolve over a long period of time, with the person slowly reacting emotionally to the growing situation; in theatre, you think of condensing the crisis, selecting the specific moments that simultaneously show the most significant aspects of the problem and the facets of the character.

Contrast

Contrasted characters give your play dynamic movement, vitality, and interest, and contrast sets each character off from the others and provides a basis for conflict. If you want to write a protagonist who has, say, moral strength, you can emphasize that quality by creating another character who is morally weak. For illustration, think of dynamically contrasting characters such as Medea and Jason in Euripides's *Medea*, Macbeth and Banquo in Shakespeare's *Macbeth*, Blanche and Stanley in *Streetcar*, Reverend Parris and Reverend Hale in *The Crucible*, or Eddie and May in Sam Shepard's *Fool for Love*. In *The Crucible*, Proctor's intense desire to do what is fair and just is emphasized by other characters who are cruelly self-serving.

The Colorful and Unconventional

The wacky character, as Lanford Wilson says, is perfect for the theatre. The delightful eccentric enlivens plays, whether the central character or a less important one. Wilson's *Hot L Baltimore* is peopled with wacky characters who make the play come to life, and Babe, the central character in Beth Henley's *Crimes of the Heart*, is interestingly unconventional (she's the one who shot her husband and then made a pitcher of lemonade).

Deciding How Many Characters You Need in Your Play

In the above discussions we indicated ways you can freely use characters to amplify and enrich your play. Now we must balance that freedom by introducing pragmatic concerns about the number of characters you use.

Essential and Nonessential Characters

A concept of economy influences most aspects of theatre, paring superfluous qualities down to their most economical statement and affecting such diverse elements as scenery and acting. It applies to characters as well. Essential characters contribute to the play's conflict and help establish or reinforce the protagonist–antagonist struggles. In contrast, even though utility characters may be convenient for the playwright—servants to answer the phone or delivery people to bring messages or the like—if they are nonessential, you should consider eliminating them from the play.

The Playwright's Juggling Ability

The more characters the playwright puts in the play, the greater the risk that he or she will be like the clown who tries to balance an increasing number of spinning plates on slender sticks, desperately running back and forth to stop one from falling while trying to add another. The clown can handle four or six plates, but after eight or so the chances of plates crashing increase. So, too, the playwright faces problems juggling a large number of characters: It's all too easy to drop a character—to forget that he or she is onstage. For these reasons it is wise to limit your play's cast size to the number you can comfortably handle and keep alive so they make vital contributions to the action.

Expenses versus Opportunities

If you are aiming at a professional production, be aware that producers look at characters as dollar signs. Because each character is an actor who must be paid and costumed, some professional producers are necessarily wary of the costs of large-cast plays (say, more than eight to ten characters).

In contrast to the professional theatre's concern about expenses, many college and high school theatres, which do not pay actors, will look for large-cast shows to increase participation opportunities for student actors. Such theatres expect that all, or at least most, characters will be richly written to challenge actors.

Small Roles

Konstantin Stanislavsky, the Russian acting teacher, once said there are no such things as small parts, only small actors. It sounds like a nice idea, perhaps valuable in building morale of those cast in walk-ons, and is often quoted by directors trying to encourage actors to concentrate on playing the one-line roles. It is also nonsense. Actors who have played spear-carriers or members of the crowd know these are small parts, thankless and uninspiring. If you have small roles in your play, ask yourself if you'd like to be cast in them.

EXERCISES

1. Write a detailed character biography of your play's protagonist, using the guidelines suggested in this chapter and adding other information you think is important. Assign the protagonist personal traits that you find worthy of respect, qualities you like in people: You want the audience to care intensely about the protagonist's needs. Be sure the protagonist is different from all other characters in the play.

2. Describe the protagonist's goal—what he or she wants—and why that goal is vitally important to the character. What makes the protagonist want that goal? What will the audience see happening to stimulate the protagonist into action? What does the protagonist have at stake? What is his or her emotional involvement? What is the protagonist doing to achieve the goal? How does the protagonist reach out to involve the audience?

3. Specify the protagonist's single basic characteristic. What are his or her secondary characteristics?

4. Identify the protagonist's emotional ranges.

5. What are the play's environments? How do they affect the protagonist? How do they influence all other characters?

6. Construct a character biography of your play's antagonist, using the guidelines suggested in this chapter. Be certain the antagonist is different from the protagonist, perhaps even directly opposite in selected significant areas.

7. Describe the antagonist's goal—what he or she wants—and why that goal is important. Why does the antagonist oppose the protagonist? What does the antagonist have at stake?

8. Specify the antagonist's single basic characteristic and secondary qualities.

9. Define the antagonist's emotional ranges.

10. Does your play need a visible objective? Describe the character.

11. Would a confidant(e) or foil help you establish the protagonist? If so, describe the character.

12. Assign each smaller character distinctly different qualities. Think of polar opposites to build contrast.

I'm convinced that there are absolutely unbreakable rules in the theatre, and that it doesn't matter how good you are, you can't break them. . . . You must state the issue at the beginning of the play. The audience must know what is at stake; they must know when they will be able to go home: "This is a story of a little boy who lost his marbles." They must know, when the little boy either gets his marbles back or finds something better than his marbles, or kills himself because he can't live without his marbles, that the play will end and they can applaud and go home. He can't not *care about the marbles. He has to want them with such a passion that you are interested, that you connect to that passion. The theatre is all about wanting things that you can or can't have or you do or do not get. Now, the boy himself has to be likable. It has to matter to you whether he gets his marbles or not.*

— Marsha Norman

ADDITIONAL READING ON THE TOPICS OF THIS CHAPTER

Linnell, Jim. *Walking on Fire: The Shaping Force of Emotion in Writing Drama*. Southern University Press, 2011. A poetic consideration of the importance of conflict and emotion in drama.

Smiley, Sam with Norman A. Bert. *Playwriting: The Structure of Action*. 2nd ed. Yale University Press, 2005. Ch. 6 "Character." An extensive and analytical treatment of the elements that make up dramatic characters.

Waxberg, Charles S. *The Actor's Script: Script Analysis for Performers*. Heinemann, 1998. Acquaintance with the manner in which actors get from page to stage can help guide a playwright's work.

Constructing Dialogue
Action through Words

> *The ear is an essential quality of the dialogue-writer, the ear that can catch and reproduce the tone of characters' speech. . . . Really good dialogue is not what it would be in life; it can only seem to sound as if it were. No stage bore can be boring the way a real life bore is. He would bore the audience, too.*
>
> — JOHN VAN DRUTEN
>
> *True words are not necessarily beautiful.*
> *Beautiful words are not necessarily truthful.*
>
> — KUNG FU TZU (CONFUCIUS)

Your characters talk.

Is dialogue nothing more than people talking? Hardly.

George Bernard Shaw, with characteristic trenchant wit (and equally characteristic lack of modesty), pointed out that if his plays are "merely talk" then Beethoven's symphonies are "merely music." Shaw accurately indicates the complex qualities of dialogue. Being a playwright requires mastering the art of writing dialogue, which is much more than people talking. Directors and audiences encounter your play's dialogue first, before plot and characters become visible, and you want to earn their favorable attention by constructing dialogue that has the same vitality and animation that you give characters and plot.

When your dialogue succeeds, the result is exciting. Hearing your dialogue onstage, delivered by talented actors and communicating effectively to an audience, is a thrilling reward that essayists, poets, and novelists can never experience.

Dialogue Is Verbal Action

A preliminary definition helps us start this chapter's exploration of the many dimensions of dialogue: *Through speeches and silences, what is spoken and deliberately unspoken, dialogue is the action that characters do.* For example, both verbal and physical actions are present in the famous "nose" scene in the first act of Edmond Rostand's *Cyrano de Bergerac.* Cyrano eloquently mocks Valvert's lack of imagination in saying, "Your nose is rather large," then duels with him while simultaneously composing a ballade—"Then, as I end the refrain, thrust home!"

Expect some mild confusion about terms referring to characters' speeches. Theatre workers often use "dialogue," "speech," and "lines" synonymously, although the first word refers to the playwright's written script and the latter two are actors' terms. Some directors and playwrights also think of dialogue as "diction," a term that reflects the Aristotelian division of drama into six elements: plot, character, thought, diction, music, and spectacle. Although theatrical dialogue means dramatic exchanges between two or more characters, common theatre practice also applies the word to monologues, soliloquies, and speeches in one-person monodramas.

Theatrical Dialogue Differs from Other Forms of Writing

Stageworthy dialogue is similar to, yet different from, speeches or dialogue in novels. As a writer you necessarily respect language and fundamental principles of good writing, such as concern for emphasis through sentence structure, use of active instead of passive voice, and appropriate word choices. As a playwright, however, you freely break writing rules to achieve theatrical effect. We can envy Lewis Carroll's egg's arrogant freedom to make words his slave—"'When *I* use a word,' Humpty Dumpty said in a rather scornful tone, 'it means just what *I* choose it to mean, neither more nor less'"—but when *we* use a word it means what the audience thinks it means, and we'd better be certain we're communicating accurately.

Most of us have three vocabularies: the spoken (the smallest vocabulary), the heard (second largest), and the read (largest). Theatrical dialogue typically uses the first two vocabularies; formal or literary writing, in contrast, involves the third. Some playwrights, perhaps interested in proving their literacy, depend heavily on the third vocabulary, and their plays contain dialogue that is stiff, stilted, distant from humanity, or even full of quotations from poems or essays. Expect directors to reject such plays.

Theatrical Dialogue versus Life's Conversations

Theatrical dialogue differs radically from life's "conversations," "discussions," "chats," or comparable terms that suggest idle, emotionless, rambling, disorganized, ordinary talk. Those qualities do not make effective dialogue for the stage. Thinking that your characters chat or talk is a red danger flag indicating you're missing the essentials of dramatic writing, which is carefully selected, individualized, condensed, shaped, and organized for characters and plot. Although you seek to evoke the flavor of the way people talk in real life so your characters will appear real, you never replicate real-life chats and instead construct their dialogue to achieve dramatic tensions and conflicts. Certainly playwrights like Chekhov and Mamet wrote dialogue that *appears* to be casual conversation, but their plays succeed because beneath the surface chatting, the subtext is lively, pointed, and frequently vicious.

Theatrical Dialogue versus Writing for Novels

Theatrical dialogue differs from dialogue found in many novels. From your reading, you know that some novelists write long, rambling speeches or lengthy descriptions as if the other players in the story somehow temporarily disappeared from the scene; novelists may use inverted or convoluted sentences on the premise that the reader has the option of rereading the passage to find its sense; and novelists can include words, figures of speech, or literary allusions that require the reader to consult a dictionary or a literary concordance.

Such writing techniques, perhaps acceptable in novels, are ineffective in the theatre. Ernest Hemingway said that the novelist is engaged in a perpetual battle to craft the perfect sentence; the playwright, in contrast, is less concerned with individual written sentences and more interested in oral communication of the entire story. You're like a storyteller crafting suspense and illuminating mysteries to a group sitting around the campfire, and every aspect of your story must be clear and interesting to everyone, aimed at neither the elite nor the unsophisticated.

Theatrical Dialogue versus Literary Writing

"Dialogue in this play sounds like literary writing," a producer or director may say about a play. It is no compliment. Often the comment explains why a play is rejected.

Theatrical dialogue is an artistic reproduction of the way particular characters speak, designed for actors to speak and aimed at the audience's ear, in contrast to literary writing which is more formal, written for an individual reader's eye. When appropriate to the character and situation, theatrical dialogue uses incomplete sentences, incorrect grammar, informal style, slang, and profanity. As a playwright your first priority is dramatic characterization and action—your dialogue shows characters in action, the opposite of a literary essayist dispassionately commenting on life.

Theatrical Dialogue versus Screen Writing

Screenwriters and playwrights share common bonds. Both are storytellers who depend on conflict for dramatic impact, seek to give artistic representations of life, use similar plot and characterization techniques, and write within the same mandate to "show, not tell." They differ in the amount they use dialogue and visual images. Screen writing, whether for television or movies, depends on visual images more than dialogue; the playwright, in contrast, depends on dialogue more than visual communications.

Theatrical Dialogue versus Speech Writing

Stageworthy dialogue is like public speaking in that both are forms of oral communication directed at the auditor's ear, but it differs from speaking in a number of significant aspects. Speech making often is oratorical and follows rhetorical rules, which makes it similar to literary writing, and it usually informs listeners or exhorts them to take action. Theatrical dialogue, in contrast, is an exchange of sharply contrasting views between more than one person, and usually without any explicit call for action on the part of the audience.

Debate, an organized form of speech, presents ideas in a logical point-counterpoint system, a coolly analytical attitude ill-suited to dramatic writing, which is full of fiery statements by opinionated individualists who won't let an opponent develop a counterargument. As a playwright, think of yourself as one who shows humans in action, not as a politician or member of the clergy who makes speeches about issues.

The Playwright's Goals

Effective dialogue must serve many functions. You seek to create dialogue that expresses the play's action and conflict, brings the characters into sharp focus, informs the audience of situations and focuses its imagination on the play's theme, communicates the play's tone, and contributes to the play's aesthetic appeal.

Dialogue Is Action

Active and vital dialogue thrusts your play forward as much as active and vital character and plot give the play forward momentum; passive or inactive dialogue slows the play's pace no less than passive or inactive character and plot. Harold Pinter's *The Dumbwaiter* deals with two professional killers arguing over apparently inconsequential matters because they are increasingly nervous as they wait for their victim to enter. They become involved in a power struggle. Ben tells Gus to light the kettle to make tea. Gus says no one can light a kettle; Ben must mean light the gas.

BEN: (*Powerfully.*) If I say go and light the kettle, I mean go and light the kettle.

GUS: How can you light a kettle?

BEN: It's a figure of speech! Light the kettle! It's a figure of speech!

GUS: I've never heard it.

BEN: Who's the senior partner here, me or you?

GUS: You.

BEN: (*Vehemently.*) Nobody says light the gas! What does the gas light?

GUS: What does the gas—?

BEN: (*Grabbing him with two hands by the throat, at arm's length.*) THE KETTLE, YOU FOOL!

Very simply, if your dialogue does not move the play's action ahead, your play will seem wordy and overwritten; if your dialogue pushes the action forward, the play will feel vital and engrossing.

Dialogue Reveals Tensions Underlying Actions

Effective dialogue is full of tension, like spiritual and psychological rubber bands stretching to a snapping point, showing conflict and people working at cross-purposes, characters' emotional involvement in issues highly important to them, and vital disagreements. Edward Albee's *Who's Afraid of Virginia Woolf?* illustrates dialogue's tensions and actions. At one point Martha goads George into attacking her, and they wrestle to the floor. While Honey shouts "Violence! Violence!" Nick pulls George off. George regains his composure and says, "We've played Humiliate the Host," and then asks what other games they can play: "How about . . . how about . . . Hump the Hostess? HUNH?? How about that? How about Hump the Hostess? (*To Nick.*) You wanna play that one? You wanna play Hump the Hostess? HUNH? HUNH?" Seeing George's desperation, Martha says scornfully, "Portrait of a man drowning."

Dialogue Makes Emotional Appeal

Dialogue conveys characters' emotions and awakens comparable feelings in the audience. "Pray you, undo this button," Lear says in the heart-wrenching conclusion of *King Lear*. At the end of Tennessee Williams's *A Streetcar Named Desire,* a doctor leads Blanche from the home of Stanley and Stella; Blanche has one of theatre's most poignant speeches that sums up her character: "Whoever you are—I have always depended on the kindness of strangers." Act One of Beth Henley's *The Wake of Jamey Foster* ends with Marshael Foster, the new widow, in despair: "I don't know how I'm gonna get through this night. I can't imagine ever seeing the morning."

Dialogue Expresses the Playwright's Credo

Dialogue can express the personal beliefs that led you to write your play. In Arthur Miller's *Death of a Salesman*, Biff sums up his father: "He had the wrong dreams. All, all, wrong. The man didn't know who he was." In Doug Wright's *I Am My Own Wife*, the playwright must decide whether or not to write his play after discovering that his central character, Charlotte von Mahlsdorf, collaborated with the Stasi. In his last visit with her, looking at some of her scarred antiques, he asks, "Does a piece ever get so old—so damaged—that you throw it away?" She responds, "*Nein*. You must save everything. And you must show it—*auf Englisch*, we say—'as is.' It is a record, yes? Of living. Of lives." And the playwright goes on to write his play.

Dialogue Implies Theme

Although you do not want to express your play's theme explicitly—a direct statement violates theatre's "show, don't tell" directive—you can imply it with subtle dialogue. *Hamlet* contains the well-known statement that describes the play's focus: "Something is rotten in the state of Denmark," followed by a less known but more significant line: "But Heaven will set it right." Rebecca in Thornton Wilder's *Our Town* shows the play's concern with universal truths when she says Jane Crofut received a letter addressed to her: "Jane Crofut; The Crofut Farm; Grover's Corners; Sutton County; New Hampshire; United States of America." Asked what's unusual about that, she adds that the envelope's address also included: "Continent of North America; the Earth; the Solar System; the Universe; the Mind of God."

Dialogue Shows the Play's Tone

Joe in William Saroyan's *The Time of Your Life* expresses the play's warmth when he talks about the marriage that he almost had and all the imagined kids, adding: "My favorite was the third one." Also in the play is an Arab who sits alone at the bar and from time to time says nothing more than two words that express the bewildering mysteries of human behavior: "No foundation." At a telling moment he expands on his idea by adding six words: "No foundation—all the way down the line." Dialogue in Oscar Wilde's comedy, *The Importance of Being Earnest*, shows the light-spirited tone with serious references to consumption of delicacies (ALGERNON: "Why is it that in a bachelor's establishment the servants invariably drink the champagne? I ask merely for information." LANE: I attribute it to the superior quality of the wine, sir. I have often observed that in married households the champagne is rarely of a first-rate brand.").

Dialogue Stimulates Audience's Imagination

Theatre becomes more effective when it awakens the audience's imagination. In Sam Shepard's *Fool for Love*, the Old Man (visible only to Eddie and the audience but not to others in the play) shows the power of the mind when dealing with love. He tells Eddie to look at a picture on the wall, although no picture is present: "Barbara Mandrell. That's who that is. Barbara Mandrell. You heard a' her?" Eddie says he has. "Well," says the Old Man, "Would you believe me if I told ya' I was married to her?" Eddie says no. "Well, see, now that's the difference right there. That's realism. I am actually married to Barbara Mandrell in my mind. Can you understand that?"

Dialogue Reflects Characters: Characters Create Dialogue

Dialogue and characterization are like love and marriage: Dialogue creates characters, and characters create dialogue. One secret for a successful marriage can be stated simply: Create characters who are compelled to say what you need them to say.

Ineffective dialogue makes characters sound stilted, bland, emotionless, uninterested and uninteresting, or oratorical. Effective theatrical dialogue brings characters to life by giving them tensions, obstacles, unique emotions, vitality, and dedication to achieving their goals. In Eugene O'Neill's *The Hairy Ape*, the protagonist is Yank, a stoker on an ocean liner. He discovers that a beautiful female passenger called him an ape who made her sick when she saw him working at the ship's boilers: "Yuh tink I made her sick too, do yuh? Just lookin' at me, huh? Hairy ape, huh? (*In a frenzy of rage.*) I'll fix her! I'll tell her where to git off! She'll git down on her knees and take it back or I'll bust de face offen her!"

Dialogue Shows Characterization

Dialogue shows your characters' individual personalities and powerful needs, relationships, beliefs, thoughts, and emotions. Often a simple speech shows the inner workings of the mind: When Macbeth tells his wife that King Duncan will arrive at their castle this night, she responds, "And when goes hence?" Four words show wheels busily turning in Lady Macbeth's mind, plans and connivances that express her character and imply forthcoming bleak actions. Macbeth later shows that in freely taking others' lives as if they were worthless he has unwittingly made his own as meaningless: "Life's but a walking shadow, a poor player / That struts and frets his hour upon the stage, / And then is heard no more: it is a tale / Told by an idiot, full of sound and fury, / Signifying nothing."

Dialogue Captures and Shows Character's Unique Qualities

Dialogue is like a fingerprint, unique for each character in your play. In this sense you apply what you learn from listening carefully to friends, relatives, and public officials. Each individual's oral style, word choice, and sentence structure makes him or her immediately identifiable. For example, as satirists and comics demonstrate, even casual followers of politics readily recognize the phraseology and style of a John F. Kennedy, Richard Nixon, Jimmy Carter, Ronald Reagan, Bill Clinton, Barack Obama, or Donald Trump.

Imagine that someone has transcribed an intense argument among your mother, father, and friend or spouse. You receive a typed copy of that scene but minus identifying names. You could identify each speaker by his or her particular emphases, use of words, and sentence structure. Likewise, all of your play's characters, or at least each major character, need individualized dialogue.

For example, the characters in Lynn Nottage's *Sweat* have individual concerns and personalities expressed through dialogue. Oscar wants a paying job, no matter what it costs him. Tracey becomes driven with racism fueled by economics. Brucie is obsessed with his drug habit. Jason's anger drags him into violence. And Stan, broken and wiser, just wants to keep the peace.

Dialogue Makes Characters Easily Recognizable

In realistic plays, each character has an individualized voice or manner of speaking. When you succeed in creating speech patterns distinct for each character, someone reading the play can recognize each speaker by dialogue alone.

Think of the highly individualized dialogue of Stanley versus Blanche in Tennessee Williams's *A Streetcar Named Desire*. Each has distinctive rhythms and words. Perhaps more important, each has highly individualized topics—Blanche talks about her appearance and ethereal subjects; Stanley speaks of raw, animalistic self-concerns.

Individuality comes with knowledge of the characters. The better you know the characters, the more you'll achieve the elusive goal of individualistic speech patterns. Contrasts are helpful for many plays: Think of each character as having a widely different background, education, environment, and employment. Give each character distinctly different emotional and intellectual qualities, ambitions and dreams, reactions to stimuli, and vocabulary. You'll discover a serendipity factor: As you continually seek to create distinctive dialogue for each character, he or she will take on added dimension, energy, and individuality.

Acquiring an Ear for Dialogue

Earlier chapters discussed the "writer's eye" for dramatic action and characters. Here we discuss what playwright John Van Druten says is an equally important imaginative tool: your "writer's ear" for dialogue to communicate your vision from the page to the stage through the actors to the audience. Effective dialogue requires the playwright to have a love for words and the way words mix to construct ideas that depict characters. An ear for language hears vitality, rhythm, word choice, speech patterns, images, and brevity. Four basic sources can help you improve your ear for dialogue: life, actors, other playwrights, and the characters and your imagination.

Life

You can train your ear by learning from life, listening carefully to speech patterns of people around you, recognizing unusual qualities, and noting how each individual expresses emotions and thoughts through unique word choice, rhythm, and sentence structure. Because you're most interested in dramatic values, be especially attentive to people in conflict over desires, ideas, and needs. Just as painters fill sketch pads with bits and pieces of anatomy or landscapes that can be used for their paintings, fill your writer's notebook with oral sketches that may later become part of a character in a play.

Actors

Another way to train your ear is to ask actors to read your play while you listen carefully to the dialogue, perhaps closing your eyes to concentrate more fully on the lines. Do they have to pause for breath in the middle of sentences? Try writing simple, declarative sentences. Do they stumble over unfamiliar terms? Consider substituting better known words. Do you hear words blending together because terminal sounds are followed by similar sounds ("seems simple," "cook can," and the like)? See if you can recast the sentence. Does the dialogue sound like an ordinary chat? Construct conflict that shows characters working against each other. It's a good idea to experiment with changing lines so you can hear the importance of rhythm, sentence structure, word choice, and images. Actors' comments and suggestions may help you strengthen your dialogue.

Other Playwrights

You can improve your ear for dialogue by studying other playwrights, attending plays in production or rehearsals, and listening to the way the dialogue is constructed. Careful play reading will sharpen your ear and increase your ability to distinguish between effective and ineffective dialogue. Some playwrights believe they learn to improve their writing skills by copying word for word other playwrights' excellent dialogue passages, not to imitate but to discover firsthand how superior dialogue is constructed.

The Character and Your Imagination

Dialogue springs from characters. Playwrights train themselves to "listen" to what each character wants to say and the unique way he or she says it. Your goal is to be sure all characters are vital and alive: When one character is talking, focus your writer's ear on the others and demand they respond. You'll find that dialogue is improved if you create characters who are so different from one another that they necessarily have different speech patterns; alternatively (or simultaneously), force characters to have different ways of expressing themselves so they'll be dramatic opposites.

Avoid Examples of Poor Dialogue

Not all examples of dialogue will help you develop your ear. Avoid inferior dialogue, such as that often found on television's daytime soaps. Your ear is ill-served by their rambling sentences, overripe and unmotivated emotions, junk words, halting speeches, repetitions, and dependency on camera tricks or sound effects to add snap and crackle to anemic lines. You don't need such qualities infecting your ear for dialogue.

Communicating Basic Details

Plays must be complete and self-contained. You use dialogue and action, not printed programs or the like, to communicate all necessary basic information to the audience. Names, situations, and relationships are the foundation stones for the play's shape and construction, and without knowledge of such fundamental materials the audience may not be drawn into the characters and situations. The larger the number of characters, and the more complex the situation, the greater effort you'll have to make to help the audience know the essential details.

Dialogue Communicates Facts, Names, and Relationships

The passage below illustrates the playwright's use of dialogue to convey basic information immediately to the audience. Note that in just a few moments the audience knows the characters' names, differences in their attitudes, and certain details about their respective pasts. Strokes of foreshadowing indicate an ominous future. The play begins with these lines:

CLIFF: (*Opening door.*) Ralph? Is that you? God Lord, what are you doing here this time of . . .

RALPH: (*Entering.*) I'm driving by on my way home, see your lights on, and I say to myself, "Self," I say, "Self, Cliffie-boy is still up. Let's say hey to good old Cliff." So, hey, Cliff.

CLIFF: (*Weakly.*) Hey, Ralph.

RALPH: (*Active, looking around room, busy.*) Ain't seen you, been a while, right? Like maybe, what, six years? Didn't you know they let me out a few weeks ago? I surely thought my old buddy Clifford W. Carpenter would look me up real fast.

CLIFF: Look, it's late and I've got a busy day tomorrow . . .

RALPH: Hard to find you. Went to your old dump and they told me you'd moved, no forwarding address.

CLIFF: Yeah, well . . . So, how have you been?

RALPH: (*As before.*) Pretty slick, this place. Books, paintings, wall-to-wall carpet, silver in the cabinet. Man, you doin' okay for a guy who six years ago didn't have more 'n fifty bucks at one time.

CLIFF: Ralph, you live, what? Twenty, twenty-five miles away?

RALPH: (*A large smile.*) You know where I live, huh?

CLIFF: I mean, what's this about just passing by?

RALPH: (*Waving his hand vaguely.*) Old buddies got to keep in touch. You 'n' me, we gotta catch up. Let's you and me get a drink outta your fancy bar and we'll bullshit about the good old times when we used to go huntin', chasin' girls, and raisin' hell.

CLIFF: (*Hesitantly.*) Ralph . . . Not a drink. Not since they put you in . . .

RALPH: (*Quickly.*) Hey, I'm cool, pal. On the wagon. This here's solid-citizen Ralph Thomas McQuire, no warrants outstanding, all bills paid to society. But you don't have to worry about society asking you to pay up, do you?

CLIFF: (*Looking at watch.*) I'd like to talk but . . .

RALPH: (*He puts his hand in his coat pocket. There is a large bulge.*) Just a couple minutes, Cliffie-boy.

CLIFF: (*Apprehensively, looking at the bulge.*) Now look, Ralph . . .

RALPH: We'll catch up on things, have one drink for old times. I thought 'bout you a lot, my old, old friend. I missed you. Six years, looking at the sun through them damned bars, I missed you. (*Smiling.*) Yeah, ol' buddy, we're gonna catch up.

The "Rule of Three" Insures Communication

How can you be confident that the audience knows vital factual information such as names, relationships, situation, conflicts, and the like? Professional playwrights emphasize a rule of three, by which they mean giving the audience important information at least three times. This rule, more pragmatic than philosophical, is based on an awareness that the audience may have problems hearing and comprehending specific details that are mentioned only once.

Note the application of the rule of three in the above Cliff–Ralph scene. Facts are repeated: characters' names, the late hour, implications about where Ralph has been, statements regarding six years (made significant in Ralph's last speech), and suggestions that Ralph may have a problem with alcohol. Different vocal patterns emphasize the contrast between the two characters.

The rule of three also applies to plot and thought. In the Cliff–Ralph scene there are repeated units of foreshadowing that indicate a troubled relationship, starting with Ralph entering without invitation, allusions to Ralph searching for Cliff who seems reluctant to be found, suggestions that Cliff has more money now than he did six years ago, and especially the repeated "old buddy" lines.

Effective use of the rule of three calls for deft and subtle writing. You want to hide the technique—dialogue will sound strained if the audience recognizes the device at work—and characters must have clear motivation for each repetition. Common sense tells you not to use names too often because that violates the way people speak and, further, would quickly become singsong. The theatre artisan will use indirect restatement more than word-for-word repetition.

Specifics Communicate More Thoroughly than Abstracts

Specific references—explicit names, locations, facts—help the audience relate to the character and situation. For example, Jane Martin's mono-drama *Twirler* focuses on a young lady's experience as a baton twirler. Martin could have written that the character's mother sent her for baton twirling lessons and let it go at that, but instead she uses concrete, specific references that give the dialogue immediacy and meaning: "Momma hit the daily double on horses named Spin Dry and Silver Revolver, and she said that was a sign so she gave me lessons at the Dainty Deb Dance Studio where the lady, Miss Aurelia, taught some twirling on the side."

Equally, the playwright might have said that the twirler had an accident, but Martin again uses the specific: "Oh, I've flown high and known tragedy both. My daddy says it's put spirit in my soul and steel in my heart. My left hand was crushed in a riding accident by a horse named Big Blood Red, and though I came back to twirl I couldn't do it at the highest level. That was denied me by Big Blood Red who clipped my wings." The specific references themselves convey an elevated feeling like poetry, giving your dialogue (and your character) added sparkle and meaning.

Pronouns Weaken Communication

Just as specific references are valuable because they communicate basic details and a sense of place, pronouns are remarkably anemic in theatrical dialogue because they lack specificity. Although you don't want to fall into the trap of unnecessary repetition, you'll find that repeating the noun is usually more effective: "Big Blood Red" is stronger than "he." Furthermore, antecedents may be lost (the novel's reader can skim backward to find the reference noun, but the listener cannot). Examine your dialogue for references to he, she, they, and it, and substitute proper names or nouns if there's any chance of confusion or if the specific conveys more power.

Techniques of Writing Dialogue

I love plays where there is actually style in the language. I like plays that have a sense of language that is exact and exciting, almost pristine in its simplicity. A play's language should have an inevitable musicality that leads to the play's emotional and intellectual center.

— Linda Hunt

It's the way the playwright thinks, the imagery, the metaphor, his or her sense of theatre, that makes me want to do a play.

— Hume Cronyn

Actors such as Linda Hunt, winner of an Academy Award for *The Year of Living Dangerously,* and Hume Cronyn, who appeared in many plays and films, reflect opinions of many other actors: They are attracted to working in a play on the strength of its language and theatrical metaphor. Directors, actors, and producers look for plays that are written for the stage, that is, with theatrical features such as action, characters in motion, visual qualities, and, most especially, dialogue that is of and for the theatre.

Ellipsis: The Unfinished Thought

You've seen the ellipsis (a series of three dots) in formal writing to indicate missing material in a quotation, but in dramatic dialogue the ellipsis indicates a character's unspoken thoughts or words. (Some playwrights prefer to use dashes instead of dots.) Perhaps the character is unwilling to face a blunt truth, or he or she may be hesitant to offend another character. Sometimes the character may struggle for words. You'd write such dialogue like this:

BILL: I think I'll . . . Or maybe not.
ANNE: If you don't do what he said as soon as . . . your father said he'd . . .
BILL: Yes, but . . . No. I won't do it!

Ellipses quickly can become overused—the above example probably has too much cagey nonstatement—but when properly used, the device can show each character's emotional and mental state.

Making Clear the Unfinished Thought

Ellipses or incomplete sentences may confuse actors, making them search for the missing meaning and perhaps coming to incorrect conclusions. To insure clarity, you can indicate the unspoken completion of the sentence. Armed with that knowledge, actors can use vocal techniques to communicate the unspoken to the audience. For example, in *Agnes of God,* John Pielmeier used the standard series of dots to indicate the ellipses and then added a parenthetical note to explain to the actor the rest of the sentence (which is not spoken):

DOCTOR: (*Laughing.*) You're as crazy as the rest of your family.
MOTHER: I don't know if it's true, I . . . (only think it might be possible).

DOCTOR: How?

MOTHER: I don't . . . (know).

DOCTOR: Do you think a big white dove came flying through her window?

MOTHER: No, I can't believe that.

DOCTOR: That would be a little scary, wouldn't it? Second Coming Stopped by Hysterical Nun.

MOTHER: This is *not* the Second Coming, Doctor Livingstone. Don't misunderstand me.

DOCTOR: But you just said . . . (there isn't any father).

The above example also indicates another device to enliven dialogue: the Doctor's satirical newspaper headline ("Second Coming Stopped by Hysterical Nun"). The capital letters and content make the sense clear to the actor, who will select an appropriate reading.

Contractions and Incomplete Sentences

Theatrical dialogue uses contractions to capture the sound of real-life people speaking naturally. Look back at the Cliff–Ralph scene and imagine the characters saying "I am" instead of "I'm," "let us" instead of "let's," "I have not seen you" instead of "haven't seen" or "did you not" instead of "didn't you." The result of such changes would be stilted dialogue at best, so ill-suited for the characters that they would be emasculated. Only the most formal characters in your play will say "cannot," "do not," or "I will," and such construction alone won't create a formal quality in the character.

Similarly, incomplete sentences, phrases, and elliptical construction often create effective dialogue. Few characters form spoken sentences with the same attention to grammatical rules as would a skilled writer.

Interruptions that Enliven Characterization

People seldom politely wait for the other person to finish a thought. More frequently they interrupt each other. Those interruptions increase with the depth of emotional involvement. As your characters become angry and upset, or delighted and overjoyed, you'll find that they want to interrupt or override each other, and the result is scenes that crackle with tension and excitement. Note the interruptions that show the characters' emotional turmoil in the following example from Tennessee Williams's *The Glass Menagerie:*

TOM: What in Christ's name am I—

AMANDA: (*Shrilly.*) Don't you use that—

TOM: Supposed to do!

AMANDA: Expression! Not in my—

TOM: Ohhh!

AMANDA: Presence! Have you gone out of your senses?

TOM: I have, that's true, *driven* out!

AMANDA: What is the matter with you, you—big—big—IDIOT!

TOM: Look!—I've got nothing, no single thing—
AMANDA: Lower your voice!
TOM: In my life here that I can call my OWN! Everything is—
AMANDA: Stop that shouting!

Physical Action to Eliminate Words

A lively sense of theatre means, among other things, being alert to the physical contributions the actors can make to express unspoken dialogue. In simplest terms, you can use actor directions to replace dialogue with physical action. Instead of writing a line that says, "Yes, I agree with you," you write the actor direction (*Nodding.*) and let the actor communicate the information. "Do you want a drink from this bottle?" can become (*Holding bottle up and looking inquiringly at him.*).

Consider John Pielmeier's use of an actor direction to replace words in *Agnes of God*. In the following passage, Mother Miriam Ruth is explaining to Dr. Livingstone how Agnes could conceal her pregnancy from others in the convent:

DOCTOR: How did she hide it from the other nuns?
MOTHER: She undressed alone, she bathed alone.
DOCTOR: Is that normal?
MOTHER: Yes.
DOCTOR: How did she hide it during the day?
MOTHER: (*Shaking her habit.*) She could have hidden a machine gun in here
if she had wanted.

Pielmeier might have given the Mother a lengthy explanation such as "All of us nuns wear large, voluminous habits that can hide most anything you can imagine," but it would have been less effective than "shaking her habit." The simple actor direction neatly eliminates excess words and uses the stage. Perhaps more important to the playwright, actor directions are part of imaginatively *seeing* characters in action while writing the play, thus helping bring them to life.

One word of warning, however: While no ethical director or actor will change or cut the words of a script, common practice is not so careful about executing stage directions. An important communication that is only expressed in a stage direction may simply be cut by an actor or director. Crucial information should, therefore, be anchored by dialogue. Notice that the shaking of Mother's habit is anchored by her words "in here." Without the business of shaking her habit, the line would not make sense.

Variety and Contrast

Variety and contrast are important tools in many aspects of playwriting, and certainly in writing dialogue. Theatrical dialogue is enlivened by variety in length of sentences and speeches, phrasing or structure, word choice, imagery, use of incomplete phrases, ellipses, and the like. Variation also creates contrast for emphasis: A series of short speeches before a long speech will make the latter stronger, and crude or mundane language emphasizes flights of poetry.

Tmesis

Certain characters may be made vivid by tmesis, splitting a word or compound phrase by an expression put between its parts, such as "absofuckinglutely" or "neverthehellless." Because it draws attention to itself, use such a device judiciously and sparingly, and because it is so distinctive, you'd likely give that technique to only one character.

Principles of Structural Emphasis

A sentence has three areas of strength: the end, which is the strongest; the beginning, second in strength; and the middle, the weakest part of the sentence. The premise of structural emphasis is that the most significant concept, word, phrase, or idea is placed at the end of the sentence, the secondary concept is placed at the beginning of the sentence, and the least important materials belong in the middle. Not all materials deserve emphasis. Use phrases for the least significant matters, clauses for moderately important ideas, and full sentences for vital concepts.

Emphasis by Structure: The End of the Sentence

An old vaudevillian joke illustrates the concept that the most emphatic emphasis is at the end of the sentence.

STRAIGHT MAN: Who was that lady I saw you with last night?
COMIC: That was my wife, not a lady.

It just doesn't work. The comic punch belongs at the end of the sentence: "That was no lady: that was my wife."

Several speeches between Amanda and Tom in *The Glass Menagerie* illustrate theatrical dialogue that uses the emphatic ending position. The following example contains two incorrect uses of emphasis at the end of the speech.

(1) TOM: I thought perhaps a gentleman caller is what you wanted.
(2) TOM: A gentleman caller is what you wanted, I thought.
(3) TOM: I thought perhaps you wished for a gentleman caller.

The first two examples (which Williams did not write) are poorly written because they don't use emphasis correctly. The two key words—gentleman caller—for this sentence and for the play receive special attention because they are at the end of the sentence in the third example (which Williams *did* write).

To illustrate emphasis in a longer sentence, examine Amanda's speech to Tom:

AMANDA: You are the only young man that I know of who ignores the fact that the future becomes the present, the present the past, and the past turns into everlasting regret if you don't plan for it!

The operative concept is "planning for the future," a key to Amanda's character throughout the play. The location at the end of the sentence gives the phrase strength.

Emphasis at the End of a Speech

As indicated above, the end of a sentence conveys the most emphasis. So, too, does the end of a speech. For illustration, note Lady Macbeth's "sleepwalking" speech (*Macbeth*, Act V, scene 1):

LADY MACBETH: Out, damned spot. Out, I say! One; two. Why then 'tis time to do't. Yet who would have thought there'd be so much blood in the old man? Hell is murky. Fie, my lord, fie! a soldier, and afeard? What need we fear who knows it, when none can call our power to account?

But that is not the way Shakespeare constructed the speech to build to a climax. The above speech is confused, muddy, and anticlimactic. This is the way Shakespeare used the climactic power of a speech's ending:

LADY MACBETH: Out, damned spot! Out, I say! One; two. Why then 'tis time to do't. Hell is murky. Fie, my lord, fie! a soldier, and afeard? What need we fear who knows it, when none can call our power to account? Yet who would have thought the old man to have had so much blood in him?

Note the differences in the two constructions of the final sentence. "Yet who would have thought there'd be so much blood in the old man?" "Yet who would have thought the old man to have had so much blood in him?" Moving "blood" closer to the end of the speech makes the second example stronger.

Emphasis by Structure: The Beginning of the Sentence

The discussion above indicates that sentence structure can create emphasis and concludes that the most emphatic is the ending. Second in power is the sentence's beginning. In *Death of a Salesman*, for example, Arthur Miller gives Willy a sentence that places the emphasis on the beginning: "Chevrolet, Linda, is the greatest car ever built." (It would have been less effective if written this way: "Linda, I say a Chevrolet is the greatest car ever built."). Later Willy says, "'Cause I get so lonely—especially when business is bad and there's nobody to talk to." (The emphasis on "lonely" would have been lost if stuck in the middle of the sentence: "When business is bad I get lonely when there's nobody to talk to.")

Placement of Proper Names in Sentences and Questions

The principle of structural emphasis also affects placement of names in sentences. If at the end of the sentence, it may cause the actor to give little energy to the speech. Read the following examples aloud to yourself and note how the sentence fades off in the first example.

"Yes, I want to go, Jim."

"Yes, Jim, I want to go."

Placement of names at the end of sentences tends to weaken the speech. The effect is perhaps more noticeable with questions. Again, read these examples aloud:

"Do you want to get out, Jim?"

"Jim, do you want to get out?"

Special Aspects of Dialogue:
Imagery and Poetry, Monologues and Soliloquies

The revolutionary newness of The Glass Menagerie . . . *was in its poetic lift, but an underlying hard dramatic structure was what earned the play its right to sing poetically. Poetry in the theatre is not, or at least ought not be, a cause but a consequence, and that structure of storytelling and character made this very private play available to anyone capable of feeling at all.*

— Arthur Miller

We associate poetic diction with dramatists such as Shakespeare and Molière as well as with twentieth-century playwrights such as Federico Garcia Lorca, Maxwell Anderson, Christopher Fry, T. S. Eliot, and other writers who use rhythm and images to bring music and song to their dialogue. In the twenty-first century playwrights such as Suzan-Lori Parks, Dan O'Brien, and Lucas Hnath have also utilized free verse in their plays. If you want that special, elevated speech, think of poetic diction as being like musical theatre: Playwrights and composers give characters songs when mere prose will not suffice.

Poetry serves much the same purposes and is used for much the same reasons. Poetic diction is effective when prose cannot express the characters' depth and range of feelings. If you want to create poetry, don't start with word choices and imagery. Think instead of characters of sufficient size who can speak in elevated language and have feelings and needs that demand poetic diction. Poetic diction begins with the situation and the characters. Sprinkling poetic language and symbols throughout the play is not a recipe for success.

Poetic simplicity often is effective, as illustrated in the following passage from Tennessee Williams's *A Streetcar Named Desire*. Blanche hopes Mitch will provide her the safe refuge she desperately needs.

MITCH: (*Drawing her slowly into his arms*) You need somebody. And I need somebody, too. Could it be—you and me, Blanche?
(*She stares at him vacantly for a moment. Then with a soft cry huddles in his embrace. She makes a sobbing effort to speak but the words won't come. He kisses her forehead and her eyes and finally her lips. The Polka tune fades out. Her breath is drawn and released in long, grateful sobs.*)
BLANCHE: Sometimes—there's God—so quickly!

Blanche's five simple words demonstrate the power of poetic diction to express characters' emotional flights. It would be jarring, however, if the playwright gave her a poetic quality only this one time. Early in the play Williams establishes Blanche's ability to speak in elevated diction, making this speech a logical part of her emotional qualities throughout the play.

Williams also uses contrast effectively. Mitch's diction is ungrammatical and clumsy, the opposite of Blanche's; and his proposal, while heartfelt, certainly is mundane enough. That contrast further emphasizes the power of Blanche's speech.

Imagery

Imagery is enhanced diction, a description that awakens the audience to a place, an action, a thing, or an experience. You may use figurative imagery to speak indirectly to the audience's imagination or literal imagery to speak directly to the audience's knowledge. Least effective in theatrical dialogue are allusions consisting of only a word or phrase; successful use of imagery in theatre requires you to sustain and develop the material.

Some playwrights construct an entire play around an image. *The Glass Menagerie*, for example, centers around Laura's collection of small glass animals, delicate pieces that represent Laura's personality and Amanda's dreams. Other playwrights may use an image once to drive home a particular idea. Jean-Paul Sartre's *No Exit* has a particularly terrifying image that begins the play. Garcin and the Valet are onstage.

GARCIN: (*Eyes the VALET suspiciously.*) I thought as much. That's why there's something so beastly, so damn bad-mannered, in the way you stare at me. They're paralyzed.
VALET: What are you talking about?
GARCIN: Your eyelids. We move ours up and down. Blinking, we call it. It's like a small black shutter that clicks down and makes a break. Everything goes black; one's eyes are moistened. You can't imagine how restful, refreshing, it is. Four thousand little rests per hour. Four thousand little respites—just think! . . . So that's the idea. I'm to live without eyelids. Don't act the fool, you know what I mean. No eyelids,

no sleep; it follows, doesn't it? I shall never sleep again. But then—how shall I endure my own company?

The Monologue

A monologue is one character's extended speech. Unlike the aside, the monologue is heard by other onstage characters, and you want to be certain they are motivated to let the speaker talk at length without interrupting him or her. The speaker also must have reasons—usually heightened emotional involvement with the topic or issue—to speak for so long. The monologue's effectiveness is proven in plays by modern playwrights as varied as Lynn Nottage (*Sweat*), Jez Butterworth (*The Ferryman*), Conor McPherson (*The Night Alive*), and Annie Baker (*The Flick*).

The Soliloquy

The soliloquy is similar to the monologue in that it is one character's speech showing deep feelings and thoughts. Distinctions between the two terms are blurred, but generally the soliloquy is spoken when no one else is onstage. Some theatre people reserve "soliloquy" for speeches that are more formally or poetically constructed than monologues; others seem to use "soliloquy" for classical plays and "monologues" for more modern works.

The soliloquy was popular in Elizabethan drama, best illustrated in Shakespearean plays such as *Hamlet* and *Macbeth*. It faded in the nineteenth century with the advent of realism, which rejected its artificiality, but in the twentieth century it came back to life in works of playwrights such as Eugene O'Neill, Thornton Wilder, and Samuel Beckett.

Dangers to Avoid

Errors can creep into dialogue, making it weak and ineffective. No list of dangerous pitfalls can apply to all playwrights and plays—what may be unsuccessful dialogue for one playwright can become a source of strength for another—but we can describe certain common dangers that you want to avoid.

Repetition

As we discussed earlier, the rule of three suggests repetition helps ensure communication to audiences, but in other instances repetition can become irritating and boring. Most dangerous are senseless repetitions of previous speeches, as indicated below:

MARK: Do you want to tell me what to do?
MIMSY: Why should I tell you what to do?
MARK: Give me a break—I need some help.
MIMSY: You need help? No way. I'm not going to help you.

MARK: Why won't you help me?
MIMSY: Help you? Look, it's not my job.
MARK: But it is your job. You're supposed to help me.
MIMSY: By telling you what to do?
MARK: Hey, you caught on!

Horrible, isn't it? That sort of repetition is valuable only if the playwright intends the audience to thoroughly dislike these two insipid characters or if the playwright is getting paid by the word. Otherwise, avoid senseless repetition which destroys the play's forward movement, makes the characters appear witless, and too easily can become a habitual way of writing.

Past Tense

Drama is an art of the present, with a lively sense of future. Past-tense verbs can drag the play out of its present into the past and deny movement toward the future. The play's focus on the present and future calls for phrases such as, "I'm doing it (now)" and "I'll do it (tomorrow)," but not "I did it (five years ago)."

If you find your dialogue contains past-tense verbs, think of them as red flags that warn of a focus on the past. A limited number of past-tense verbs are almost essential to allow characters to show the relevance of their past to their present and future action. A large number, however, indicates you should ask yourself if your play might be better if you transfer the action to the past.

Junk Words

"Oh," "well," "so," and "yeah" are junk words with little nutritional value. Typically found at the beginning of speeches, such words more likely come from the playwright than the character. Not only do they weaken speeches but they also cause actors to soften their attack on their lines. Perhaps writing such words may help you get characters to speak during your initial stages of constructing the play, but during the revision process you should look carefully at junk words to see if they can be deleted. Most can.

Clichés

Clichés lack originality making them especially inappropriate in playwriting. Although you may deliberately give a particular character trite expressions to show his or her mundane thought processes, the device should be used sparingly and judiciously. (You don't want the audience to conclude the clichés personify the playwright!)

Sibilants

A series of words that contain hissing sounds can become hurdles that trip actors. They won't enjoy the challenge you give them by carelessly writing phrases such as "his zeal is zero," and you won't enjoy listening to them slow down to get through the problem as they focus more on avoiding a hiss (or, more unfortunately, a whistle) and less on character and interpretation.

Long and Complex Sentences

"Bill, that tire will have to be changed now because tomorrow noon, I must tell you, despite any objections you may have (and I was told by Sally that you'll have many), is the deadline for filing that paper I told you about last month: the application for our marriage license, which will have to be approved by the board of health."

Whew! Try reading that aloud on one breath, making sense of it while also showing the speaker's emotional attitude. Tough job, isn't it? The sense is clear, more or less, to the reader's eye. But what about the listener's ear? And the actor's problem reading it? Yet that line actually appears in a play (charity suggests we let the author remain anonymous). Can the dialogue be revised? Certainly. Start by getting rid of the passive voice in the first, parenthetical, and last phrases. Then eliminate nonessential words and express the emotion simply. Perhaps your revision may read like this: "Damn it, Bill! Fix the tire and go apply for our marriage license. Now!"

Consider the actor. Actors approach long sentences with trepidation, concerned that breath and energy may fade before they get to the end. No specific number of words defines a long sentence, but as a general rule it is perhaps twelve or more words. Yet more worrisome for actors are complex or convoluted sentences that twist and turn like snakes, burying the essential meaning. The more phrases and inversions, the more difficulty the actors will experience; the more problems they have, the greater the likelihood they won't read the line as effectively as you'd wish.

Simple sentences. Note that most examples of effective theatrical dialogue in this chapter are simple, direct sentences. Actors' apprehensions do not necessarily argue for a play containing only short sentences, which could become boring for the playwright to write, the actor to speak, and the audience to hear, but you do need to think of the actors' problems as you construct dialogue. Here is yet another reason you should read your play aloud, revising sentences that create problems for performers.

Long Speeches

Related to long sentences are long speeches, a common flaw in many plays. There are no guidelines suggesting that, say, three to four sentences per speech are acceptable but more than five fall into dangerous territory, but your writer's ear helps you recognize that long speeches can become windy, slow the play's pace, or exist for the playwright's convenience and not the characters' needs. One fears that often a speech is long simply because the playwright didn't cut and revise.

In special cases, however, long speeches can be powerful if the character is highly motivated. For example, "The Story of Jerry and the Dog" from Edward Albee's *Zoo Story* is a brilliant *tour de force*; and Blanche's speech about the deaths at Belle Reve is an emotional outburst that fits the play and character. The key is character motivation and emotion. Long speeches, we might conclude, are effective when used with restraint and then only if the character is compelled to speak at length.

Ask yourself the following six questions when you've written speeches over three or four sentences long:

- Do other characters want to interrupt? If so, give them opportunity to express their emotions, developing their characters. If they remain silent, their characterization is weakened.

- Does the long speech express a single idea, or are there several ideas uncomfortably shoved together? (Look out for phrases such as "and furthermore.") A good rule of thumb is for one speech to contain only one idea; a second idea is better expressed in a second speech.

- Is the character emotionally motivated to hold forth at length? If so, the long speech may be correct.

- Are there many long speeches throughout the play? Ask yourself if the play's pace suffers.

- Do the long speeches contain exposition, playwright's explanations, or other information that is better shown in action? If so, force yourself to revise the speeches.

- Are the long speeches evidence that the playwright is not disciplined? Are the speeches a writer's self-indulgence? If so, the remedy should be evident.

Working with Actors and Directors

Your collaborators in art are the theatrical directors, actors, and designers who bring your play to life in a process that directors call "transferring the play from the page to the stage." As directors and actors will tell you, dialogue must be *stageworthy*, appropriate for theatre's unique requirements: You combine the craft of writing with the craft of oral speech aimed at the listener.

Focus on dialogue should not make us forget that theatre is an intensely visual medium, especially today. Modern audiences speak of going to *see* a play, in contrast to the Elizabethans who are described as "an assemblage of ears" because they went to *hear* a play. You therefore think of dialogue accompanying what the actors *do*.

Stage Directions

Stage directions allow the playwright to speak directly to those involved in the production—actors, designers of scenery, lighting, costumes, and sound, and especially to the play's director, who has the responsibility of artistic unification of all effects. You use stage directions to communicate your vision of the environment, characters' mannerisms and physical appearance, various special effects involving lights and sound, and activity on the stage, and actors' stage business.

While late nineteenth-century and early twentieth-century plays utilized extensive stage directions, more recent practice holds them to a minimum. Playwrights should generally avoid stage directions that tell actors how to speak their lines. Stage directions such as "angrily," "lovingly," or "her heart hardened by his rhetoric in spite of the sincere feeling behind it" should be eliminated. Usually playwrights insert such stage directions because they mistrust their own ability to put the appropriate emotion into a speech or because they mistrust actors' abilities to understand the lines and render them meaningfully onstage. If you must write such prompts in your first draft, examine them carefully in the revision process and eliminate most of them.

Memorization

In the premiere production of Samuel Beckett's *Waiting for Godot*, the actors had major memorization problems, apparently as lost in the words as Beckett's characters are in the universe. The play's repetitions are difficult to memorize and keep in order, and many similar lines make it all too easy for actors to mistake cues, leading them to leap forward or backward in the script. Neil Simon's *Brighton Beach Memoirs* has two relatively identical exchanges between the brothers, structurally similar enough to make actors start the first scene but slip into the second.

Your consideration of the actor's problems should lead you to be wary of repeating identical exchanges at various parts of the play because the stress of public performance may cause an actor to leap from one such part to a distant other. Dialogue that has a natural, logical, cause-effect flow is easier for the actor to memorize. Not unimportantly, it is easier for the audience to comprehend.

Offstage Dialogue

Offstage dialogue presents problems to actors and directors because audiences hear and comprehend speakers who are visible more easily than those who are invisible. Furthermore, actors may lose characterization if they must labor to make offstage dialogue audible through the muffling effect of scenery. Good theatre practice suggests that you use few, if any, offstage speeches. Those that are absolutely essential should be brief, easy to understand, and relatively unimportant to the plot or characterization.

EXERCISES

1. Use the following as a springboard and write four to six pages of dialogue between these two characters.

   HEATHER: (*Quietly.*) Is it time?
   SALLY JO: (*Looking nervously at the door.*) Not yet.
   HEATHER: Don't be afraid.
   SALLY JO: But they said . . .
   HEATHER: Shhhh.

   When you've finished, check the dialogue to be certain you've

   a. used the rule of three to establish the time, place, and action,

   b. made each character's dialogue unique,

   c. communicated each character's goal and emotions,

   d. avoided overly long sentences or speeches, and

   e. given the dialogue snap and crackle. Read through the dialogue to eliminate as many words as possible. Add actions to replace words.

2. Remove two major characters from the play you're writing, put them in a new situation, and repeat the above exercise. Write four to six pages of dialogue, then revise as necessary.

3. Examine ten pages of dialogue you have written and make the following changes, admittedly quite arbitrary but presented here for you to use as an experiment.

   • Force yourself to delete at least ten to twenty words per page. Does that improve the dialogue?

   • Find at least one place per page where you will substitute physical actions for words. Do you think that makes the dialogue more interesting?

   • Revise at least two speeches per page so they do not contain grammatically correct sentences but instead are unfinished thoughts or phrases. Does that give the dialogue a better flow?

   • Require at least two interruptions per page. What does that do to the characterization?

   • Force yourself to increase the emotional tonality of several of the protagonist's speeches. Does that seem to improve the character?

4. Select any play you admire and copy (by hand or on a keyboard) a page of its dialogue. What do you learn about the flow of its dialogue? Then try to revise that page. Do you find places where revisions would be absolutely wrong? Or other places where revisions may help the dialogue? What qualities make the differences?

5. Go to a place where you can eavesdrop on conversations without getting in trouble for doing so. Listen to a conversation for ten minutes or so. Don't use a tape recorder. Immediately afterward, go somewhere and do your best to write the conversation as accurately as possible. Don't try to correct or improve the conversation. What do you learn about how people talk?

6. Make an audio recording of a conversation between you and your friends. Listen to it later and maybe transcribe it. What do you learn about conversational speech? What would you have to do to shape this conversation and the one in exercise 5 into dramatic dialogue?

Howard Lindsay has said, and very rightly, that a couple of lines can make a scene too long, four lines make it very much too long, and six can make it impossible. You would not have thought that cutting four lines out of a scene can make much difference. I have done it, and I know it can. . . . Cutting, and a willingness to cut, are two things that can serve a playwright best. . . . Few plays have been damaged by cutting, and most have been improved. I am talking now of cutting not only lines, but words.

— John Van Druten

ADDITIONAL READING ON THE TOPICS OF THIS CHAPTER

Castagno, Paul C. *New Playwriting Strategies: Language and Media in the 21st Century.* 2nd ed. Routledge, 2011. Multiple chapters deal with contemporary dialogue practices (e.g., "Crossover Poetics: Sarah Ruhl and Suzan-Lori Parks" and "Foundations of Contemporary Monologue").

Smiley, Sam with Norman A. Bert. *Playwriting: The Structure of Action.* 2nd ed. Yale University Press, 2005. Ch. 8 "Diction." A detailed treatment of dramatic dialogue.

8

Laying the Groundwork for Production Elements

> *You cannot say . . . that such and such is not a play because it violates the unities or is in one long act or has a speech of ten pages' length. But you can say, for example, that when a dramatist—as I remember to have seen once in a manuscript—writes that the heroine turns and walks out the door at the back of the room and as she reaches it smiles a radiant, happy smile, he may be writing fiction but is not writing in theatre terms, since the audience could not see at all the smile, which therefore as theatre it does not exist.*
>
> — STARK YOUNG

As the quotation from legendary theatre critic, teacher, and playwright Stark Young demonstrates, playwrights need a lively sense of *stage realities* in order to write effective plays.

This chapter focuses on the playwright writing stageworthy scripts. We have already discussed plays as *stageworthy* in contrast with scripts more suitable for cinema, fiction, or television (See chapter 2 and elsewhere). Now we will consider writing plays that clearly take into consideration theatrical realities and that prepare the way for the other theatre artists to bring our scripts alive—*on stage.* Theatrical elements we will cover include casting; design features, such as costume and makeup, scenery and props, lighting and sound, and various staging modes; and the physical placement of performers in relationship to the audience.

Playwrights need to develop the fundamental impulse while writing to visualize the action of their plays taking place on stage, not in "reality."

As Aristotle wrote in his *Poetics*, "In constructing his plots and using diction to bring them to completion, the poet should put the events before his eyes as much as he can. In this way, seeing them very vividly as if he were actually present at the actions, he can discover what is suitable." How can playwrights develop this theatrical vision? First, by seeing and reading as many plays as possible and then by taking theatre classes—classes in acting and stagecraft in particular. Playwrights can also profit from auditioning for roles in plays and from working on stage crews in academic or community theatre productions. Even small acting roles and serving on props crews will give the aspiring playwright insights into stage processes—what works or doesn't work and new ideas for staging plays.

Production Elements for Playwright Consideration

Casting

We have already discussed characterization, the dramatic considerations that go into creating the people in your script (See chapter 6), but now we need to look at related theatrical realities and, in particular, cast size. A quick look at the cast lists of a play by Sophocles and one by Shakespeare quickly suggests that different periods of theatre history have called for different sizes of casts. Sophocles was provided only three speaking actors, and all roles had to be played by those three. In contrast, Shakespeare had to provide roles for a dozen colleagues, none of whom were female. In the twenty-first century, economic realities have returned us to a period of small casts. Professional theatres must provide actors a living wage, and touring theatres need to fit their cast and crew into a van. Yes, there are a few plays like Jez Butterworth's *The Ferryman*, which has a cast of 21 plus an infant, but such plays are rarities unless the playwright is aiming for high school or collegiate theatres where actors are not paid and many student actors need roles. But even in these theatres, every additional actor adds at least one more costume, and actors in walk-on roles still have to show up for almost as many rehearsals as those in principal roles.

In short, a cast size much over six may limit your play's chances for production. As a rather popular solution to this limitation, some playwrights utilize cast doubling in order to increase the number of characters in their plays without increasing the cast size. In some cases there may be a few actors assigned to individual, major roles with a small ensemble of actors who each plays a variety of minor roles. Lisa Kron's *Well*, for instance, calls for two actresses who play Lisa and her mother Ann plus an ensemble of two men and two women who play all other roles. And Eric Overmyer's *On the Verge* requires three central actresses plus a male actor who plays multiple roles. J. T. Rogers's *Oslo* has a huge character list—17 plus walk-ons—but its Broadway premiere was performed by a cast of 14 with considerable doubling. While doubling may be done to keep cast sizes manageable, as a by-product, many audience members find it theatrically interesting as they watch actors take on different roles right before their eyes.

As you plan your play, look for ways to keep your cast small and consider whether the drama and theatricality of your play might be enhanced by ensemble doubling.

Finally, if you are writing for a particular theatre, consider the diversity of their acting pool as you populate your play. Actors Theatre of Louisville, for instance, had one of the foremost ten-minute-play festivals in the country; however, their ten-minute plays were performed by their apprentice company, so they would not consider plays for that festival that included characters outside the 18- to 30-year-old range.

Design Elements: Costumes, Makeup, Scenery, Props, Lighting, and Sound

As you visualize your play *on stage* (remember—not in "real life") while you write your script, you will see characters being performed by actors who are wearing costumes provided by a designer and costumers, handling props created by property technicians, living their lives on sets designed and built by scenographers and shop crews, under lighting that comes from a variety of well-placed, properly focused instruments, against a background of sounds and music selected and executed by sound designers. While it is the designers' privilege and responsibility to create these details, it is your duty and your right as playwright to lay the foundation for their work.

Which begs the question, how many specifics are enough for you to include in your script, and how much is too much? As a rule of thumb, playwrights indicate the basic requirements of these elements and the effects they visualize, but they leave the specifics up to the designers. In this way, playwrights insure that the fundamental demands of their plays are covered while permitting the designers full freedom to bring their admirable talents to bear realizing the play on stage.

Consider the following initial stage direction of Ibsen's 1879 play *A Doll's House* as a sample of an outmoded, overdone set description:

> *A room, comfortably and tastefully, but not expensively, furnished. In the back, on the right, a door leads to the hall; on the left another door leads to HELMER's study. Between the two doors a pianoforte. In the middle of the left wall a door, and nearer the front a window. Near the window a round table with armchairs and a small sofa. In the right wall, somewhat to the back, a door, and against the same wall, further forward, a porcelain stove; in front of it a couple of armchairs and a rocking chair. Between the stove and the side door a small table. Engravings on the walls. A whatnot with china and bric-a-brac. A small bookcase filled with handsomely bound books. Carpet. A fire in the stove. It is a winter day.*

Few twenty-first-century playwrights would preface their plays with such an extended, specific set description, and if they did, they could expect that designers would simply ignore the stage direction. How might a current playwright describe the set? First, we already know from the play's cast list and setting page that the play takes place in Norway in the late nineteenth century. What set description might work to convey the necessities and the atmosphere while giving the designers freedom to create? Maybe something like this:

> *The central living room in a middle-class apartment. It is tastefully but not expensively furnished—comfortable, even cozy, with a feminine touch clearly in evidence. Doors open to HELMER's study and to the hall which leads to the flat's front door. A winter day, near Christmastime.*

This brief description permits the initial script reader to visualize the scene. Everything else that the designer needs to know is clearly indicated in the play's action. Working with the director, the designer will determine what furniture items to provide, where to locate the doors and furniture, the colors and set dressings, and so on.

Descriptions of costumes, props, lighting, and sound can follow these same principles: include what is necessary, indicate the desired effects, and leave the details to the director and designers.

What about multi-setting plays, costume changes, and the like? Avoid plot structures that demand set changes between scenes. Most set changes demand at least a full minute, and that minute will seem like an eternity to an audience which is forced to sit in the dark or watch the stage hands move scenery while they wait for the play to continue. If you must place scenes in more than one location, find ways to facilitate transitions without set changes.

A similar approach might well be utilized for scene-to-scene changes of costume or makeup. If an actor needs to be on stage at the end of a scene in one costume and then appear at the outset of the next scene in a different costume or makeup, the audience may again face an extended wait while the changes are made. Some playwrights expect designers and technicians to solve such matters, but wisdom suggests that, if the playwright can facilitate the change, the result may be even more satisfactory. Some current plays have costume changes being made onstage in full view of the audience. In other cases, a playwright may find a dramatically believable reason for an actor who must make a costume change to leave the stage before the end of a scene and come on a page or so after the onset of the next scene.

Finally, notice that extensive (and expensive) design demands may either keep your play from being done or may result in a stripped-down version that you will find disappointing. No theatre is going to construct a realistic imitation of the Taj Mahal for your ten-minute play. Not every theatre has a turn-table, multi-batten fly system, trap room, closet full of scenic projectors, or elevator stage to accommodate your vision. Keep it simple. If a theatre wants to add bells and whistles, they'll do so.

Placement of Performers and Audience Members

Different theatres have different configurations of their stages and audience areas. For a century or more, the proscenium stage has been standard. But the twentieth century saw the advent of arena stages and thrust stages. Occasionally some theatres utilized environmental staging with performance areas interspersed amongst audience seating. And some theatres performed plays in found spaces not originally designed for performances. To accommodate this variety, some theatres have adaptable spaces that can be reconfigured for each play. Each of these architectural arrangements places the audience in different relationships to the performers.

While most plays can be produced in any of a variety of theatre arrangements, some seem to demand specific staging. The arena staging of Peter Shaffer's *Equus* so clearly fits the action and thematic impact of that play that proscenium theatres that present it almost always position some audience bleachers on the stage facing the auditorium across the acting area. In contrast, Anthony Shaffer's *Sleuth* almost demands proscenium staging in order to mask the equipment that produces its gunshot effects.

Consider the best audience/performer relationship for your play. Visualize that arrangement while you write, and if it is important to the play's action, include it in the set description on your script's introductory pages. But be aware that any given theatre may or may not utilize the staging you designated. Conversely, if you're writing for a particular theatre, visualize their stage arrangement as you write.

Staging Modes

Related to these production elements, plays differ in their staging modes. Some of these differences have to do with historical theatrical styles—classicism, romanticism, realism, expressionism, epic theatre, absurdism, or postmodernism. Some have to do with influences from other world stages—Kabuki, Noh, or Sanskrit drama. Some have to do with presentational versus representational modes or differences in theatrical conventions such as the utilization or rejection of the fourth wall.

As a twenty-first century playwright, familiarize yourself with these different staging modes by reading plays and theatre theory books, taking theatre history classes, and attending a wide variety of plays. While much of this book focuses on writing action-based plays in a realistic mode, current theatre practice accepts and even encourages a wide variety of styles. Avoid being different just for its own sake, but exercise the freedom to utilize different modalities that fit your script's action and themes.

Insuring Theatricality

If a script will make a good movie or TV show, it doesn't belong on the stage.

— Edward Albee

As Edward Albee's stark statement suggests, something about the stage makes live theatre different from its cinematic and electronic cousins. That essential feature is the simultaneous presence of the performers and the audience—live actors presenting a play in the presence of live audience members. Even if the play observes the fourth wall so that it *appears* that the actors don't realize that hundreds of people are watching them, everyone—audience members and performers alike—realize that the actors are very much aware of the spectators. The immediacy of theatre, then, gives a stage play a unique, paradoxical impact. On the one hand, the audience/performer encounter is absolutely real—an audience member who walked onto the stage could reach out and touch an actor. On the other hand, both actors and audience members participate in a complex game of make-believe—the actors pretend to be characters other than themselves, and the audience pretends to believe the same fiction. That paradox—simultaneous reality and fiction—gives theatre its special nature and sets it apart from movies and television.

Plays for the stage should realize that paradox and exploit it. In other words, stage plays should be *theatrical*. They should use the juxtaposition of appearance and reality to impact the audience.

How do you make your play theatrical? Playwrights, directors, and designers have experimented with many ways to theatricalize the stories they have presented onstage. We will note a few of these techniques here, but certainly others exist and more will be created as theatre moves into the future.

Plot devices can provide theatrical impacts. The ancient Greek playwrights included choruses who interacted with the characters and commented on the action. Current plays such as Suzan-Lori Parks's *Father Comes Home from the Wars* bring back this convention. Other plays insert narrative moments that may present background information or accent the play's emotions and meanings. For instance, in J. T. Rogers's *Oslo*, characters frequently turn abruptly to the audience to introduce new characters or present background information: Early in Act 1, Mona turns to the audience and says, "To clarify: Johan Jorgen is married to Marianne, who works for Terje, who is married to me, who, as of tomorrow, works for Johan Jorgen. In Norway we take nepotism to an entirely new level. It's a very small country and we think and behave as such," at which point she rejoins the scene in progress. Additionally, songs placed within otherwise "straight" plays can have choric impact as is the case in Parks's play.

Some plots utilize episodic structures or manipulate time by means of nonlinear plots with flashbacks or leaps ahead. Lynn Nottage's *Sweat*, for instance, frames its central action, which takes place in 2000, with prologue and epilogue scenes that take place in 2008. And Doug Wright's *I Am My Own Wife* and Dan O'Brien's *The Body of an American* jump back and forth throughout time and space. Scenes can also simply segue from one to another without blackouts or other punctuation as in Mark Medoff's, *Children of a Lesser God.*

Characterization and acting styles can also provide theatricality. We have already discussed monodramas, in which single actors play multiple characters, and plays that utilize ensembles or doubling of roles. Some plays like *Equus* or Timberlake Wertenbaker's *Our Country's Good* situate "offstage" actors in full view of the audience, and Sam Shepard's *Fool for Love* places a character not central to the play's action onstage and has him interact occasionally with the principals. Numerous plays eliminate the fourth wall and have characters frankly acknowledge the presence of the audience, address the audience directly, or even leave the stage to interact with audience members.

Dialogue presents unlimited opportunities for theatricality. While much of our treatment of dialogue has focused on techniques of realism, we have also noted that some plays are written entirely in verse or scatter verse or songs throughout the action. Paul Castagno's treatment of dialogic plays in his *New Playwriting Strategies: Language and Media in the 21st Century* identifies, defines, and discusses numerous other striking approaches to theatrical diction. Additionally, some plays utilize projected titles, as advocated by Bertolt Brecht, to accent the impact of scenes. Lynn Nottage, for instance, begins each scene of her play *Sweat* with its date, the day's weather, and headlines from the national and local news.

Sound cues of all sorts can also contribute to a play's theatricality. Pre-show and background music can set and modify a play's mood, voice-overs can impact action, and sound effects—realistic or otherwise—can communicate to the audience. Even as old and realistic a play as Chekhov's *Cherry Orchard* utilized the sound of a breaking violin string to emphasize the death of the old retainer Firs at the end of the drama.

And of course, visual design elements have long been used for their theatrical impacts. Samples of visual design approaches to theatricality include open staging, unit sets, and nonrealistic, abstract, or symbolic costumes, makeup, props, and lighting.

Notice that the presentation style of a play should usually be introduced very early in the first scenes so that the audience is prepared for what to expect. All of the action in Lucas Hnath's *The Christians*, for instance, is staged at the front of a church sanctuary utilizing microphones. Even scenes that would have occurred in the pastor's study or with his wife in the privacy of their bedroom are presented in this setting. The play begins with a choir singing two hymns as the pastor and his wife enter. This beginning clearly sets the presentational style of the play. In contrast, Dario Fo's *We Won't Pay! We Won't Pay* moves through most of its action clearly observing the fourth wall—until the very end when suddenly the actors break character and deliver a harangue to the audience, driving home the play's message. While the playwright clearly intended the shock provided by this change in theatrical mode, some audience members found it just too unnerving. It's probably wiser to set the rules of your play early and stick to them.

Danger Areas

Because of the essential nature of theatre, some elements that film audiences accept without batting an eye have a much different impact on stage and should therefore be approached with caution.

Many audience members have become accustomed to partial or complete nudity in movies, but onstage nudity seems to have a more shocking impact. Of course there are plays like *Oh, Calcutta!* that are performed largely in the nude, and audiences who purchase tickets for these shows come well prepared for what they will see. And plays like *The Prime of Miss Jean Brodie*, *Hair*, *Equus*, and *Angels in America: Millennium Approaches* make judicious and appropriate use of nude scenes. But impact on audiences and the concerns of many theatre producers are such that new playwrights may well think several times before including nudity in their plays.

Depending on where one lives, works, and plays, one may hear frequent or constant use of what might be called "gestural language"—profanity and obscenities. While legal censorship of public obscenities is fortunately a thing of the past, and while the aim of realism may call for strong language, nevertheless, obscenities and profanity on stage tend to have a stronger impact than in real life or in film. Generally speaking, a little obscenity goes a long way in creating the effect of realism, so new playwrights might be well advised not to overdo it. A useful approach might be to include whatever gestural language seems appropriate in drafting the play, trim it a bit in revisions, and then observe audience responses carefully during readings to make certain the language furthers the play's impact rather than calling attention to itself.

Sex and violence also have a different impact on stage than in film. Here's the difference: while film has always tried to present such events in all their shocking reality, theatre does better at revealing the *meaning* and *impact* of the events. Meaning and impact are better served by showing what leads up to the event and what follows it in the lives of the characters than by depicting the blood and guts. Showing graphic details of sexual acts or violence onstage can so jolt an audience that they overlook the dramatic meaning of the event. Remember—live audiences are watching live actors execute these actions. If the performances are exceedingly realistic, the audience may fear for the well-being of the actors; if the acts seem intended to be real but look fake, the audience may find them laughable. Neither response is likely to further the play's impact.

Understanding Stage Directions

Article I of the Playwright's Bill of Rights circulated by the Dramatists Guild of America reads "No one (e.g., directors, actors, dramaturgs) can make changes, alterations, and/or omissions to your script—including the text, title, and stage directions—without your consent." While most ethical producers, directors, and actors would agree with this article as it applies to a play's title and dialogue, common theatre practice is less scrupulous regarding stage directions. On the other hand, some theatre professors are reputed to tell their directing, design, and acting students to take a marker and black out all stage directions before ever reading a script. This approach goes overboard in the opposite direction.

Clearly the amount of stage directions in scripts and the attitudes toward them have changed radically over the years. A brief history of stage directions will clarify the reasons for those changes—reasons that are based in changing theatre practices and artistic tastes.

Through much of theatre history prior to the nineteenth century, plays had very few stage directions. In fact, so few were they that many theatre people can quote them: "Faustus revealed in his study"; "Exit pursued by bear." There were few stage directions because they were not needed. Plays were done by tradition, so Shakespeare's company learned how to do his plays from him and those who followed them learned the roles and presentation modes from their predecessors. And the general population didn't read play scripts any more than most Americans read TV scripts, so stage directions weren't required to tell the casual reader what to envision. Furthermore, classical tastes put little emphasis on things that stage directions designate—matters of costume, vocal tonality, or styles of gesture. People in those periods were more interested in universals—what is true of most people in most places in most times, things like honor, ambition, jealousy, love, and vengeance.

As the nineteenth century dawned, things were changing. First, Europeans and Americans became more aware of historical differences and began to take them more seriously. They began to take interest in individual peculiarities, matters of personal style, unique differences—matters that stage directions can designate. Furthermore, the general populace began to read plays instead of just attend them at the theatre, thus the need for clarification of visual details. As the century progressed, melodrama became the dominant form, and melodramas called for many special effects and specific visual details that had to be conveyed through stage directions. And as the century wore on, realism became the dominant style, a style that placed great importance on heredity and environment.

Stage sets provide the characters' environments, so playwrights used stage directions to make those settings clear. As a result, by the dawn of the twentieth century, plays had lengthy, detailed stage directions similar to the initial set description in *A Doll's House* quoted earlier in this chapter.

The twentieth century saw the rise of the director, and each director strove to put his or her individual mark on each production of a script. Actors and designers shared in this desire to bring their own creative interpretation to each character, each costume, each setting. These artists tended to believe that extensive, detailed stage directions deprived them of their creative freedom. Playwrights generally profited from these creative impulses on the parts of their theatre colleagues because each production of their plays could be new and original. As a result, as the twentieth century drew to a close, stage directions became fewer and less specific.

Which brings us to today.

What is a playwright to do, then, about stage directions? As indicated earlier in this chapter, playwrights are well advised to indicate the effects they want but to leave the details and execution to the director and designers. In terms of acting, stage directions and character descriptions that indicate what the audience sees are usually fully acceptable while ones that indicate characters' internal emotions, vocal tones and volume, or specific mannerisms are best avoided or embedded in dialogue.

Writing Like a Theatre Practitioner

As you write your play, remember that you're not just a storyteller, no matter how high a calling that may be. You are a storyteller who is also a man or woman of the theatre. While you may work at your desk on your computer, your true home is the stage, and your brothers and sisters are the actors, technicians, designers, and directors who work there.

As you write your play, envision not real life but rather the theatrical event that will take place on that stage. As you write your play, focus on the event that will take place between the performers and the audience.

Now go write!

EXERCISES

1. Attend a play. Take particular notice of what makes it different from a movie, television drama, or sitcom. One place to start: a movie or a television show will crop the picture so you can see only what the camera sees while a play permits the audience to look wherever they want to look. Make a list of other differences you notice.

2. Take a script you have written. Choose three or four ideas from this chapter's section "Insuring Theatricality" and consider adding them to your script.

3. Using another short script you have written, divide it into 3 to 7 episodes. Give each one a title and notice its page numbers. Write each episode's title and page numbers on a separate 3" x 5" card.

   • Choose one card and eliminate it

   • Think of a scene to add and write its title on a new card.

   • Think of a monologue that might be spoken by one of the play's characters. Give it a title and write the title and speaker's name on a new card.

   • Think of a song that one of your characters might sing—either an existing song or one you might write. Write the song's title, along with the singer's name on another card.

   • Think of a brief dance routine that might be added to the play. On another card indicate the nature of the dance and which characters would perform it.

   • Now shuffle your cards and observe the order. There's a good chance you can come up with a better order than this random one, so put the cards in a better order, but do not return to the original order of scenes.

   • What do you have now? What might be worth keeping? What simply won't work? What have you learned about your play?

   • Using your discoveries in this exercise, revise your play.

At the time of Kean . . . *naturalism was dominant—that fourth-wall theater where you eavesdrop on something intimate and passionate. The conventions of theater that had existed for centuries were gone— the aside, the soliloquy, the poetry. Aristotle said there were six elements in the theater—not just the three of plot, theme, and character used in naturalism, but also poetry, music, and spectacle. In musicals, all six elements were brought back into the theater. . . . It interested me to be able to use all those elements. I found naturalism to be boring.*

— Peter Stone

ADDITIONAL READING ON THE TOPICS OF THIS CHAPTER

Ingham, Rosemary. *From Page to Stage: How Theatre Designers Make Connections between Scripts and Images.* Heinemann, 1998. A revelation about how designers work.

Smiley, Sam with Norman A. Bert. *Playwriting: The Structure of Action.* 2nd ed. Yale University Press, 2005. Ch. 9 "Melody" and ch. 10 "Spectacle." Details of theatrical sound and staging from the playwright's perspective.

Evaluating and Revising Your Play

> Come Blow Your Horn *was eight weeks in the writing, three years in the rewriting, and it had at least eight producers before I ever saw it on a stage.*
>
> — NEIL SIMON

Your play is finished!

Or is it?

Probably not. Although a self-congratulatory party certainly is in order to celebrate completing the first draft of your play, you must now prepare for the crucial next step: revisions. Experienced playwrights say, "Plays are not written but are rewritten," because revising your play is at least as important as writing it, and the revision process often makes the difference between a script that is performed onstage and one that never leaves the page.

Neil Simon, perhaps modern theatre's most frequently produced playwright, spent three years rewriting one of his highly successful plays. Simon's experience is not unusual. Eugene O'Neill's diary shows he worked five years rewriting and revising *Mourning Becomes Electra* from start to production version, and he expected more revisions when he heard the cast read the script. Arthur Miller spent two years revising *All My Sons*. Tennessee Williams wrote at least half a dozen drafts of his works before showing them to others; one started as a film script called *The Gentleman Caller* and went through numerous revisions over several years before it became *The Glass Menagerie*. Virtually every professional playwright has similar stories about rewriting.

We hope it will not take you as many years to see your play staged. (You can shorten the process if you start with short monodramas or one-act plays instead of full-lengths, and aim at local theatres and workshops instead of Broadway.) Still, it is safe to conclude that if O'Neill, Simon, Williams, and Miller had to spend two or three years revising (and revising and revising) a play until it met their goals, other playwrights can expect that revisions will be a complicated process. You'll want to cultivate what we might call the "Three P's for Playwrights"—perseverance, patience, and persistence. Prepare yourself mentally and emotionally to rewrite your play and allow ample time to do a thorough job.

You start by shifting mental gears from the creative mode to a careful analytical technique to evaluate your play. Your goal is to find your play's strengths, which you want to enhance, and its weaknesses, which you must correct. The revision process can be divided into three parts: accepting the idea that rewrites will improve your play, working alone in the privacy of your work space, and working with others.

The Revision Process for All Writers

The most essential gift for a good writer is a built-in, shockproof shit detector.

— Ernest Hemingway

The single most important component of an effective revision process can be stated simply for all writers: Accept the fact that revisions are essential. Never ignore rough, awkward, or incomplete places in your script, thinking that they don't matter. They do.

You need to face a blunt truth: The playwright who refuses to revise has little chance of surviving theatre's realities. Rewriting simply comes with the writer's territory; accepting that fact decreases the difficulties that are caused by reluctance to revise.

Keep the First Draft to Yourself

All writers know that they should never show a first draft to anyone. The first version simply isn't ready for exposure, and the writer's pride in his or her craftsmanship forbids letting anyone see a manuscript with flaws. Think of the responses you'll receive if you do show that initial version to someone. Will that reader's comments be helpful? Probably not: The reader won't be able to overlook rough areas to find the essence of the play. Will the reader's responses be harmful? Quite possibly: Comments that focus on mistakes can damage the writer's morale. Think, too, of the reader who sees a flawed first draft: Will he or she be eager to see later versions? Not likely.

Despite your understandable delight that you've completed a draft of your play, before you share your play with others you must first be sure it says precisely what you want it to say, neither more nor less, and in exactly the way you want to say it. Vladimir Nabokov made the point vividly: "Only ambitious nonentities and hearty mediocrities exhibit their rough drafts. It is like passing around samples of one's own sputum."

Put the Play Aside to Let It "Cool"

Playwrights often put their completed plays aside for a period of time, believing a cooling-off period allows them to return later with a more dispassionate objectivity that makes revisions easier. Experiment with this technique, but avoid letting the play sit so long that you lose interest in it. In his influential work *On the Poetic Art*, the Roman poet Horace counseled playwrights to set their work aside for eight years before sending it out. With all due respect for Horace, eight years is too long. A week or maybe two weeks is about right. You need enough time to get a bit of perspective on the play, to get past that initial rush of joy at finishing the first draft, an emotional high that often brings with it the hunch that you've just completed the next Pulitzer Prize winner. You don't want to wait until you lose all interest in the project.

Working Alone to Revise Your Play

For three years Painting Churches *was about a girl coming home and having her mother make a dress for her debut as a pianist. For three years I struggled and struggled, writing eight drafts which weren't bad, but they didn't work. Finally I got the idea that the girl would be a portrait painter and was coming home to paint her parents' portrait. It was a moment of blinding awareness, an epiphany. And everything fell together. That's how we playwrights work.*

— Tina Howe

Where do you start revising? How do you evaluate your script? What parts of the play should you examine? No one revision system can be correct for all playwrights, but a key to successful revisions involves a step-by-step method that will help you look at your script objectively. Here we discuss analytical approaches you may find effective.

Read the Play Aloud to Yourself

Your first step is to read your finished play aloud to yourself. The key is "aloud." A play is designed to be spoken aloud by actors—quite a different process from reading it silently to oneself like a novel. As you read, become the characters, imitate actors you'd like to perform the roles, stride around the room, shout the explosive lines, whisper the tender moments, and experience the emotions. Read it straight through so that you get a sense of its progression. Don't stop to make revisions or even to make notes. With your pencil, put a check mark in the margin beside items you want to examine and perhaps revise later. Soldier on through the play.

Try to avoid looking for minor changes at this point. You aren't worried about a sentence here or a speech there. Instead, look at the overall effect of the play. Having completed this first reading, ask yourself questions and make notes about the answers. What do I want to say? Is the play's meaning clear? Does the play have a unifying thread, shown by the characters in action? Is the conflict real and genuine? Is there enough action? Does it need more complications? Does it take place in the present, moving toward a future? Are there slow scenes that ought to be changed? Are the scenes in the correct order? Do the scenes build, increasing tensions?

Read Aloud Individual Characters

After reading the entire play aloud, check characterization by going through the full play and reading aloud only one character at a time. Start with the protagonist and then repeat the process with each other character. Are they all drawn as thoroughly and richly as you want? Does each respond appropriately to stimuli from other characters? Does each character evolve and change? Are the characters different from one another? Does each have individualized dialogue and consistent characteristics? Reading each character will help you revise the script. Repeat the process as many times as necessary until you cannot find areas to revise.

Continue the revision process utilizing the revision checklist at the end of this chapter. Start with large matters and, once you're certain the plot, characterization, and ideas are as you want them, then polish the writing and proofread the play—carefully. At this point, you're ready to move on to the next step.

Working with Others to Revise Your Play

Put yourself in a position where you can get your plays made public. Not that they'll always be fully performed, but at least done in classes where they'll be read out loud. Go public as soon as you can. Don't turn up your nose at coffeehouse productions or high school readings. Get out there and get it down. Don't harbor plays in your trunk. Doing them whets your appetite.

— A. R. Gurney, Jr.

Theatre is a collaborative art that is based on sharing different talents to achieve a mutual goal. Working with actors and directors helps you revise your play, puts you in close contact with collaborators, and makes you think of your play as a stage piece. Your contacts with local community, regional, or educational theatres will help you find actors and directors who are willing to participate in developing a new play. Characteristic of the generous nature of many theatre artists, actors and directors often will be eager to contribute their talents.

Have Actors Read the Play to You

When you've finished revising the play as best you can, put the script in the hands of actors and ask them to read it aloud for you. Let the play stand on its own. Avoid directing the actors; don't tell them how to interpret the characters or the lines; evade their questions about the play or the characters. Instead, encourage actors to use their creative insight to show you what *they* see in the play and the characters. Mark the play for revisions as they read. Consider audio recording the reading for future study in the privacy of your quiet work space.

Often the readings will help you find areas that need shortening. Christopher Durang, for example, said an early reading of his *Sister Mary Ignatius Explains It All for You* showed him ten minutes that "screamed out, 'Cut me. Cut me.'" At other times you may discover that your play has lost sight of its goal. Lillian Hellman said that quiet readings helped her refind the focus of *The Little Foxes*.

When the actors finish reading, invite their comments and questions, guiding them to speak primarily about characterization and dialogue, which they know well. Actors can give you insightful comments about character motivation, awkward or confusing dialogue, and the characters' biography and history. Listen to critiques without interrupting them or becoming defensive. Your responsibility at this point is not to clarify your play for the actors but rather to obtain and record their perceptions—especially the points at which your play confuses them. Take notes to show that you care about their observations. Look over the notes later when you are more objective. Revise the script and then ask the same or different actors to read the revised play. Repeat the process until you cannot find revisions.

Two additional suggestions for these readings: First, choose your actors carefully. The more experienced your actors, the more clearly their reading will show you your play's strengths and weaknesses. Avoid casting your nontheatrical friends who may be enthusiastic about helping you but who will bring no acting experience to the task.

Second, consider inviting a small audience to sit in on one of these readings. Now is the time to invite your nontheatrical friends as well as some experienced theatre folk. You want audience-based responses to the script, so selectively invite people who will give you insights from that perspective. At the end of the reading, ask a friend with theatre experience to emcee a brief feedback session so that you can take notes.

Improvisations Help Writing and Revising

As you work with actors and directors, ask them to help you explore aspects of your play with improvisational experiments (improvs), which are rehearsal techniques actors use to probe character and develop situations by going beyond the written dialogue and plot. Improvs can help you enrich and sustain scenes, add dimension to characterization, find areas that lack sufficient material, and see ways to substitute action for words. Well-guided improvs start with the script and depend on the actors already having a firm grip on characterization.

We can illustrate the value of improvisations with a small scene. Suppose, for example, you are writing a play that has two lovers who have been fighting. You plan for the male to leave. Your scene ends like this:

BETH: You can leave now.
DUFF: All right, damn it, I will go.
BETH: Good-bye.
DUFF: I . . . I—Oh, hell. (He exits.)

From the readings you may decide that the scene lacks richness. The characters' emotions are thin. Duff's exit seems rushed. The scene needs to be sustained and amplified. You can get the actors' insight in the scene by asking them to improvise how they feel, using physical activities, as well as words. They may show you something like this:

BETH: You can leave now.
DUFF: All right . . . (*He starts toward the door, pauses, looks back at her, waiting for her to speak. She doesn't.*) Damn it, I will go. (*He doesn't move.*) Beth . . . ?
BETH: Good-bye.
DUFF: (*He marches to the door, stops again, not looking at her.*) Is that all you can say—just good-bye?
BETH: Look, buddy, you've used me for the last time. I'm sick of you.
DUFF: Damn it!
BETH: Good-bye.

Perhaps the director says Beth's line about being "used" is awkward and not powerful enough to motivate Duff to leave. Ask the actress not to use the speech you wrote. Possibly she'll improvise an action similar to this:

DUFF: Is that all you can say—just good-bye?
BETH: (*She purses her lips to kiss him from the distance, then smiles at him, a big, radiant, artificially bright smile.*) See ya, sailor.
DUFF: Go to hell. (*He exits.*)

Here we looked at only a few lines in a short scene. Expand on this single example to use improvs to help you with longer scenes that appear wrong.

Ask a Trusted Theatre Expert to Critique the Script

By now you have revised the play perhaps five to ten times and are ready to ask for a detailed critique from a theatre expert such as a playwriting teacher, a director, an educational theatre professor, another playwright, or an actor. Persistence may be necessary because such people often are reluctant to critique something as personal as a playwright's work and some may not want to expend the rather large amount of time necessary for a thorough critique. You may be able to overcome their reservations by telling them what you've done to revise the play to this point and showing them that you will respect their comments. Let those insights help you revise the script again.

Evaluate the Evaluations

Expect actors, directors, and playwriting experts to give you more suggestions than you can use. Some actors and directors—and especially audiences at readings—get so involved with critiquing an original play that it becomes like a popular sport that unfortunately lacks viable rules. Evaluate the evaluations. Start by listening dutifully to the comments. Avoid becoming argumentative but mentally reserve the right to accept or reject comments according to their value to you and your play.

Some comments will seem more "here's the play I wish you'd write" and less "here's a response to the play you wrote." Those are easily rejected. Better critiques contain specific information, questions, and suggestions that will help you revise your play. Listen imaginatively and focus on what the critic is attempting to say but unable to put into words. Pay special attention to areas that bother several respondents.

Ultimately, however, this is *your* play, and only you can decide what changes to make. You may even echo George Bernard Shaw's truculent rejection of comments:

> I am quite familiar with the fact that every fool who is connected with a theatre, from the call boy to the manager, thinks he knows better than an author how to make a play popular and successful. Tell them, with my compliments, that I know all about that, that I know my business and theirs as well.

(Or perhaps you ought to delay quoting Shaw until you achieve a reputation similar to his.)

"Script-in-Hand" Reading

You'll learn a great deal about your play from a script-in-hand reading, which is presented without production values such as scenery or lighting but with well-cast and rehearsed actors and performed for a small audience. Carrying the script allows the actors to focus on characterization and dialogue; because they have scripts, you are free to revise up to the last minute without worrying if they have time to memorize new material. If the play is presented on several nights, audience reaction can show you areas to revise. Test the new material in front of a new audience.

Workshop Productions

Slightly more advanced than script-in-hand readings, workshop productions may be simple or complex. Actors will have memorized their roles, and a director will have rehearsed them to achieve the play's values. Production values usually are limited; seldom will there be scenery or costumes other than what the actors can supply from personal wardrobes, and lighting may be simple illumination. The lack of production values places more focus on the script itself, and audience response will be enlightening. You'll find more areas to revise.

Who Will Give Your Play a Showing?

Locating organizations willing to do script-in-hand or workshop productions of your play is difficult but not impossible. Chapter 11, Resources for the Playwright, tells how to find them. In metropolitan areas you'll find a number of theatres and organizations that regularly present workshop or showcase productions. In smaller towns turn to educational, community, or dinner theatres. If you work in a local theatre, you ought to be able to recruit actors and a director, and together you can convince management to set aside an evening for a small production. You can always form your own group of playwrights and actors, perhaps meeting at someone's home or using local library or church facilities.

A Checklist of Questions
to Consider at Each Step of Revision

Ultimately, the script has to answer the questions the actors have. If the answer is not in the script, then something has to be done. Rewriting Mass Appeal *was educational. I learned a lot about writing, getting the point down to the bone, making the line as spare and right as possible.*

— Bill C. Davis

"Every book, director, and playwright tells me that I'm supposed to revise," said a playwright at a national theatre workshop. "It's frustrating to be told that repeatedly but never be told *what* I should look for in my play. How do I know what to revise?" Other playwrights at the meeting agreed. The complaint is valid.

Here we list basic questions to help you evaluate your play. Use the questions selectively—not all will pertain to your particular play—and let this checklist help you create additional questions.

The Play's Overall Effect

These questions deal with the "feel" of your play, the overall impression it creates.

- What do I want to say? Where does the play achieve that goal, and where does it miss?
- Is the play true to itself? Does it achieve what it sets out to do?
- Does the play's intensity show that it represents something deeply important to me?
- Is the play's action plausible, possible, and probable?
- Is the play credible? Do characters have motivations for their actions, or are they obviously the playwright's puppets?
- Does the play have intrigue? Does it make the audience want to know what will happen next?
- Does the play have a sense of urgency that forces action to happen now, not yesterday or tomorrow?
- Is the action set in the present, not the past?
- Does the play have a sense of future?
- Is there enough surprise in the play?
- Is the play theatrical, requiring production to come to life?
- Is it compressed, or does it seem overextended? Should scenes be cut? Enlarged?
- Does the play exploit dramatic situations?

Plot Structures

A play's structure often is difficult to analyze because character and dialogue capture one's attention. The following questions help you focus on the structure of your play's action.

- Is there conflict? Is it clear? Is it sustained?
- Does the structural action of the play enhance, emphasize, show, and reflect the play's overall meaning?
- Does the play start with mood-setting? Can that be eliminated or reduced?
- Is the establishing event clear? Is it linked to the point of attack?
- Is exposition heavy-handed? Is one character forced to deliver exposition in large chunks? Does the character *need* to say an expo-

sition speech? Can I delete it or make it more subtle? Can exposition be delayed until later in the play?

- Does foreshadowing draw the audience's attention to future action?
- Can I revise the play so it starts *in medias res?* Would starting in the midst of things improve the play's dramatic tension?
- Would the play be improved with an earlier point of attack?
- Does the point of attack change the course of action?
- Is the point of attack adequately sustained?
- Does the point of attack stimulate characters (especially the protagonist) into action?
- Does the point of attack pose the play's major dramatic question (MDQ)? Is the MDQ clear?
- Is the point of attack followed by another complication that reflects and enhances the beginning of the action?
- Are there enough complications, obstacles, reversals, and discoveries? Is each adequately sustained and developed?
- Do entrances and exits create complications? Do they change the course of action?
- Are entrances and exits sustained and exploited?
- Do entrances and exits defuse ongoing conflict? Should the characters stay onstage longer to enhance the action?
- Does the play's overall action make the play grow?
- Is the climax linked to the point of attack?
- Does the climax answer the play's major dramatic question? Is the answer clear?
- Does the play end? Or merely stop?

Plot: Beginning, Middle, and End

Often you can get a strong concept of your play's effect by thinking of its beginning, middle, and end as separate parts.

The beginning

- Is the play's beginning compelling? Is it interesting? Will it make audiences want to see the rest of the play?
- Does the tone of the beginning indicate if the play will be comic or dramatic?
- Will the audience know each character's name?
- Do the characters immediately show a distinguishing quality that makes them easy to remember?
- Do I use the rule of three to repeat vital information three times to insure clear communication to the audience?

- Is the play's establishing event clear?
- Is exposition subtle?
- Does the point of attack have sufficient impact? Is it adequately sustained? Does it clearly change the play's course of action? Does it change the existing sense of equilibrium?
- Does the opening help the audience understand possible directions the action make take?
- Am I satisfied that the play's protagonist has a goal that the audience can recognize?

The middle
- Is the play's protagonist forced to struggle to achieve his or her objective?
- Does the protagonist have sufficient struggles?
- Count the number of complications (reversals, obstacles). Am I satisfied there are neither too many nor too few?
- Do entrances and exits add to the action?
- Is each complication adequately sustained?
- Does each complication change the course of the play's action?
- Are the complications all part of a master action?
- Does the middle contain surprises that are nonetheless appropriate?
- Do the characters change and evolve during the action?
- Am I certain that the play has only one climax?
- Is the play's climax appropriately sized to the struggle, neither too small nor too large?

The end
- Does the ending coincide with showing the outcome of the protagonist's goal?
- Does the ending supply an answer to the major dramatic question? Is that answer clear? Does the answer link to the protagonist's goal?
- Have I avoided *deus ex machina* devices to end the play?
- Have I avoided an O. Henry ending?

Characterization

The following questions deal with your play's characterization. Three categories help you focus on the protagonist, antagonist, and all characters.

The protagonist
- Do I intend my play to have a protagonist? If so, does the action make clear who the protagonist is?

- Does he or she appear early in the play?
- Is the protagonist directly involved with the point of attack?
- Does the protagonist have a visible, dominant, active goal?
- Is the protagonist strongly motivated to pursue the goal?
- Is the goal deeply important to the protagonist?
- Is that goal clear to the audience?
- Do actions make clear what he or she wants?
- Does the character have emotional and intellectual involvement with his or her goal?
- Does the protagonist have a plan to achieve the goal?
- Is that plan clear to the audience?
- Does he or she respond appropriately and dynamically to obstacles, reversals, and setbacks?
- Do I want the audience to like the protagonist? To respect him or her? If so, have I achieved my goal?
- Is the protagonist's goal one that the audience will approve?

The antagonist

- If I have a protagonist, is there an opposing force?
- Is the antagonist clear to the audience?
- Does the antagonist have visible, clear, strong reasons to oppose the protagonist?
- Is the antagonist's goal clear?
- Does the antagonist take enough action to oppose the protagonist?
- Is the antagonist–protagonist relationship clear to the audience?

All characters

- Do the characters (at least the primary characters) change and evolve during the play? Are the characters different because of the action they've undergone?
- Are the characters interesting? Can they be made more compelling?
- Are all characters essential to the play? Can one or more be eliminated? Will the play be tighter if I combine several characters into one?
- Do the characters have emotions? Are those strong, primary emotions? Are they clear to the audience?
- Are the characters different from one another? If they are similar, can contrasts give them added dimension and increase the tension and action of the play?
- Does each character have motivation for what he or she says and doesn't say, does and doesn't do?

- Does each care about what he or she is doing and saying?
- Do I want the audience to like one or more characters? Dislike specific ones? Does my play achieve that goal?
- Does each character have a reaction appropriate to each stimulus?
- Do the characters appear to have a life outside the universe of the play? Do they exist only for the play's structure, or do they have a life that goes beyond the play's walls?
- Are there thankless roles, such as purely utilitarian characters? If so, are they genuinely essential to the play or should they be eliminated?
- Does each character want to say each speech and do every action? Or do they appear to say or do things merely for the playwright's convenience?

Dialogue

Dialogue often is the most noticeable element of your play. The following questions direct your attention to aspects of dialogue.

- What can I delete? Can I substitute one word for four?
- Is the dialogue colorful, containing images, figures of speech, elliptical phrases, interruptions, active verbs?
- Does the dialogue have enough variety? Are there variations in length of speeches?
- Is the dialogue speakable?
- Does it come from the character?
- Is the dialogue theatrical (that is, a selected and artistic reproduction of these particular characters' speech), or is it literary (that is, designed less to be spoken and more to be read silently like an essay or novel)?
- Is the dialogue constructed with active, present-tense verbs? Can I change past-tense references to present action?
- Does each character have his or her unique speech patterns?
- Is each character's speech his or her own, or do they all speak with the playwright's tongue?
- Are long speeches (say, more than three or four sentences) essential?
- During long speeches, are there stimuli that should make other characters speak? Should they break in to express their reactions?
- Do long speeches reveal character, promote plot movement, and come from the character's driving need to speak at such length?
- Are sentences too long for the actor to handle? Can such sentences be shortened?
- Does the dialogue flow easily from the actors' mouths? Are there words or lines that make the actors stumble?

- Does the play contain dialogue that seems to indicate I want to be viewed as intellectual or well read? If so, can those speeches be revised or eliminated?

- Do speeches start with junk words, such as "well" and "oh"? If so, can I delete such words?

- Do speeches suffer from repetitive or rephrasing statements that merely echo what another character just said?

- Have I thoroughly proofread my play in order to eliminate embarrassing typos and errors in spelling, grammar, and syntax that will cause readers to doubt my seriousness as a writer?

The Play's Intellectual Core

What does your play mean? What is the intellectual core, the sum of all action and character movement? These questions help you discover if your play communicates the desired meaning.

- Does the play's title imply something important about the play's meaning? Is the title subtle yet evocative?

- Does the protagonist's goal aid the audience in perceiving the play's meaning?

- Is a major dramatic question established at the point of attack and concluded at the climax? Does that question reflect significant aspects of the play's meaning?

- Does the total action of the play add up to indicate the play's intellectual core?

- Does the play's conflict suggest the play's meaning?

- Is there a linkage between establishing event, point of attack, protagonist's goal and plan, conflict, and the climax? Do these pieces fit together? Should they be clarified or made more subtle?

- Have I avoided a curtain speech that speaks directly to the play's meaning?

Desired Audience Response

Playwrights face a number of paradoxes. One is the dichotomy of intent: On one hand, you write the play to please yourself, but on the other, your play should be aimed at a particular audience. Here you ask questions designed to help you consider audience response.

- For whom is my play written? Describe the ideal audience, thinking of age, education, level of sophistication, and the like. Examine the play through that audience's eyes. Do I find areas to change?

- What theatre do I have in mind? Is the play intended for college theatres? High schools? Community theatres? Broadway? Religious institutions? Does my play appeal to that theatre?

- If an excellent critic I respect saw a production of my play, what review would I hope to get? Does my play measure up to that review? What should I revise to be sure a critic will respond as I want?

- What is my desired audience response? State it briefly, clearly, and without fence-straddling or other equivocations that the play is all things to all people. Does the play achieve my intended response?

- What can I revise to achieve that desired audience response? Do all aspects of the play combine to create that response? Are any counterproductive? If so, can I eliminate them?

- Do I intend the audience to see my play as a comedy? Drama?

- Where in particular does my play achieve that response? Where does it miss its target?

- Will the play offend the sensibilities of some audience members? Does that bother me?

The writer's intention hasn't anything to do with what he achieves.
The intent to earn money or the intent to be famous or the intent to
be great doesn't matter at the end. Just what comes out.

— Lillian Hellman

ADDITIONAL READING ON THE TOPICS OF THIS CHAPTER

Cohen, Edward M. *Working on a New Play: A Play Development Handbook for Actors, Directors, Designers, and Playwrights*. New York: Limelight, 1997. Wisdom from a professional producer with vast experience developing new plays.

Kahn, David & Donna Breed. *Scriptwork: A Director's Approach to New Play Development*. Carbondale: Southern Illinois University Press, 1995. New script development from a helpful, director's perspective.

Lerman, Liz & John Borstel. *Liz Lerman's Critical Response Process: A Method for Getting Useful Feedback on Anything You Make, from Dance to Dessert*. Liz Lerman Dance Exchange, 2003. A widely used approach to feedback sessions that will take the fear and loathing out of the audience response process.

10

Script Format
Typing Your Script for
Producers and Directors

Walk through your local grocery store and observe the packaging. Notice the graphics, the choice of packaging materials, and the size and shape of the packages. Consider the engineering, the design factors, and the effort and expense that has been put into the packages. When you prepare your script to send out to theatrical producers, directors, agents, or publishers, you are packaging your product. A slovenly document or one that ignores industry format standards will tell readers that this playwright is an amateur who either does not know about theatrical expectations or does not care about them. The script has two strikes against it before it even steps up to the plate. On the other hand, a carefully prepared script that embodies industry format expectations suggests to readers that, whatever else may be the case, this writer understands professional standards, and your script is off to a good start. Here we describe general and specific expectations to help you prepare your play to send out. They are the standards by which your physical script is judged.

General Guidelines

You want your typed play to show a professional's care and pride in workmanship: If the play's overall physical appearance looks professional, you've started convincing readers that the play itself is excellent. Therefore you'll want to use professional writers' standards. These guidelines are relatively common for all writers.

Typing Your Play

Typeface. Use Times, Times New Roman, or a similar font with serifs. Avoid sanserif fonts like Geneva or Helvetica. Use a readable font size, usually 12 point. Never use script fonts or other decorative fonts.

Margins. Your goal is a script that appeals to the eye. Use white space so the pages won't be full of dark type. Allow one inch for the top, bottom, and right margins. The left margin should be about one and one-half inches to permit binding. Do not justify the right margin. Do not center the lines on the page.

Paper. Use normal quality copy paper. White, never colored. Print the script on one side of the paper only, never back-to-back.

Binding. Never send a script out with the pages loose or paper-clipped together. Very short scripts may be bound simply with a single staple in the upper left hand corner. Longer scripts may be three-hole punched and placed in report covers.

Proofread!

Use your word processor's spelling and grammar checking functions. Then proofread your script carefully to catch errors your spell checker will overlook, like confusions of "there," "their," and "they're." Correct all errors before you give it to anyone. Spelling and grammatical errors are not acceptable. The second or third misspelled word in your script gives readers the right to conclude you have no pride in your craft, and they may return your play unread. Play readers such as producers' assistants, agents, and contest judges, who must evaluate hundreds of plays in a brief time, face the uncomfortable responsibility of finding reasons to reject plays. Errors in spelling, grammar, punctuation, or script format give them sufficient reason. Furthermore, errors signal a careless writer, and experienced readers know that someone who is careless in writing may be unreliable in other ways as well.

Exceptions. The only exceptions to this rule are deliberate misspellings or grammatical lapses, such as when you write dialect or indicate a character's individualistic way of pronouncing words (for example, "I ain't gonna do it" or "I'm jist a-sittin' 'n' a-thinkin' 'bout it"). You can violate grammatical rules within dialogue (but not elsewhere), providing incorrect grammar depicts the character. Don't deceive yourself; readers can tell immediately if a grammatical or spelling error is a character detail or a playwright fault.

Specific Guidelines for the Playscript

We can always hope that a great play will be recognized regardless of its typed form, but you must remember that your play is one of literally hundreds submitted to producers, directors, and agents. No playwright wants to risk rejection simply because the script isn't typed correctly. Here we discuss specific elements of proper form, then use sample pages from a play to illustrate the application of typographical format.

Basic Reasons for Script Format

Understanding the rationale for a particular playscript format will help you apply the system to your play. The following reasons underlie the standard form.

- Your typed script is intended for producers, directors, designers, and actors who will bring your play to life onstage; therefore you use the typographical form that they prefer. For example, the standard script format allows estimation of the play's playing time (one typed page roughly equals one minute of time onstage), and other typographical devices help production personnel quickly find information they need.

- Ignore the formats you see in play anthologies, because those publications are designed for readers, not production personnel. The publisher's printed style is designed to save paper and printing expenses, not to help those involved in the staging process.

- Tradition is important (although not necessarily always good), and professional theatre workers expect playwrights to use the standard typographical style that they've learned to believe is best. Some believe that a play typed in any other format suggests that the playwright lacks a basic knowledge of theatre, leading them to doubt the value of the play itself.

Preliminary Pages

The preliminary pages consist of title page and the page(s) for cast of characters, time, and place. These pages are not numbered.

Title Page

The first page gives the play's title, centered and in all capital letters and italicized, plus a brief statement about the length (that is, A One-Act Play or A Three-Act Play). The author's name, also centered, is under the title. At the bottom of the page indicate copyright information (on the left side of the page) and author's mailing address, email address, and phone number (on the right side). Never send out a script without your contact information unless the submission specifications require scripts without playwright information to facilitate a blind selection process.

Cast, Time, and Place

The second page lists Cast of Characters (names, brief descriptions, and relationships if pertinent) and short statements about the Time and Place. Each of these three titles is typed in all capital letters, italicized, and centered. For a multi-act or multi-scene play, describe time and place for each act or scene.

Pagination

Never ever send out a script without its pages numbered!

Page numbers are placed in the upper right-hand corner of each page. Some playwrights also include a key word from the title. Page count begins with the first page of the actual script, not counting preliminary pages such as title or cast pages.

Pagination for full-length plays. A full-length play or multi-scene play uses a combination of Roman and Arabic numerals to indicate act, scene, and page. For example, correct identification of the first act, first scene, and third page would read: I-1-3. I-2-15 indicates first act, second scene, fifteenth page; II-1-52 indicates second act, first scene, and fifty-second page. Note that the final number (52 in the last example) always is the total number of pages; don't start recounting with each new act or scene. If your play has only one scene in the act, omit the middle number (that is, II-52). Utilize the running header and pagination system of your word processor to number your pages.

Pagination for one-act plays. For a one-act play you simply number each page consecutively without Roman numerals. A one-act play with more than one scene, however, may utilize the same system as a full-length: 1-20 indicates the first scene and twentieth page; 2-21 indicates second scene and twenty-first page.

The Script Itself

Please be patient here: Describing the script's typographical style makes the process appear more complicated than it actually is in practice. You need to learn how to use only three basic devices: indentation, line spacing (double or single), and capitalization (all capital letters or capital and lowercase).

An Invisible Middle Vertical Line

Imagine an invisible line that runs vertically down the page, three and a half inches from the left edge of the paper. That line is the left margin for stage directions and character names. Set a tab there.

Spacing. Set your word processor on single spacing. Some word processors have a default setting that adds an extra space every time you hit the enter/return key. Override this feature; you do *not* want all those extra spaces on your page.

The only time you double space is before a new speaker designation.

Stage Directions

Indentation. Stage directions are the playwright's communication to directors, actors, designers, and technical personnel, such as for lighting and sound. They are indented to the vertical line described above. Stage directions are single spaced. They are usually placed in parentheses, and some playwrights italicize them.

Don't use "stage left" or "stage right". Never write "left," "right," "center," or other terms referring to the stage's geographical areas, because that infringes on the responsibilities of directors and designers. They, not the playwright, decide what's stage left and right. They design the set according to their needs, artistic vision, theatre's architecture, and budget. Your job is to say where it happens in the play's world, not on the theatre's stage. It's fine for you to use stage directions to say a character "walks to the window," but don't write that he "walks to the down left window."

Similarly, use all capital letters whenever you write instructions to actors describing what they're doing or wearing and the like. Capital letters draw the actor's attention to that material:

> SMITH jumps under the bed when he hears the explosion. Then he yells and jumps back up, mumbling, shaking his head. SMITH'S fingers are in a mousetrap. He manages to get free and puts his fingers in his mouth.

Characters' Names to Identify Speakers

Indentation. Identify speakers by typing characters' names before their dialogue. Indent to that vertical line tab that you set for stage directions. Some playwrights center each speaker identification, but it's much easier to simply use the tab. Type the speaker's name in all capital letters. A double space separates each name from the preceding material, whether dialogue or stage direction.

Selection of the name in speaker's identification. Most characters have first and last names, even titles, but typing the full name is busywork. To identify the speaker of dialogue, select one name that best represents the character. For example, Oscar Wilde uses Algernon instead of Algernon Moncrieff, and Gwendolen instead of Hon. Gwendolen Fairfax, but he writes Miss Prism instead of Prism, basing decisions on the characters' personalities. Your word processing program may have a handy time-saving device that enters names at the press of a single selected key.

Capital letters. Use all capital letters when the character name appears in stage directions or the heading that indicates who is speaking. Use caps and lowercase when the name appears in dialogue.

Some writers put a period at the end of stage directions "(Smiling.)" but others don't.

Single and Double Line Spacing

Stage directions and dialogue are single-spaced. Double-space before speaker identifications. Single-space between speaker designations and actor directions or dialogue. Double-space after dialogue or stage directions before the next speaker's name.

Continuation of Speeches

What do you do if a character's dialogue spills over to the next page? You have two choices. First, if the dialogue creates only half a typed line on the next page (called a "widow"), don't spill over. Instead, move the entire speech to the next page. Second, if the dialogue creates more than one typed line on the next page, simply type the character's name and "continued"—SMITH (continued)—at the top of the page.

Script-Writing Software

Several software products are available for playwrights who find them preferable to formatting their own scripts. Some, like Final Draft (finaldraft.com) can be purchased and others like Celtx (celtx.com) are free. The commercial products may permit a limited time free try-out period. It is wise to try the software before investing in it. Make certain that its stage-play format is indeed in line with the industry standards sketched out above. Also make certain that it will permit scripts written on it to be saved in a variety of word processor formats; many producing organizations require scripts to be submitted as MS Word documents or in PDF format, so make certain the software you use will comply.

Sample Pages from a Script

The following pages show the application of most of the standards regarding script format. You understand, of course, that this published version can't totally replicate a typed manuscript.

TOMORROW IS TOO LATE

A Two-Act Play

By

J. T. Playwright

710 West Elm Street
Town, State, and Zip Code
Email Address
(Area Code) Phone Number

TOMORROW IS TOO LATE

CAST OF CHARACTERS

MARY LOU QUINCY. 36. OWNER OF FLIGHT SCHOOL AND FIXED BASE OPERATOR

SWASH BUNKER. 32. NEW YORK THEATRE PRODUCER

HECTOR CUNNINGHAM. 33. MECHANIC AT QUINCY FLIGHT SCHOOL

THE TIME

The action of the play takes place in the present in spring.

THE PLACE

The action of the play takes place in the interior of a flight school in Alacasta, Mississippi.

Act One.   Scene one. Quincy flight school. Morning

Scene two. Quincy flight school. That afternoon.

Act Two.   Scene one. Quincy flight school. The next morning.

Scene two. Quincy flight school. That evening.

TOMORROW IS TOO LATE

ACT ONE

Scene One

SETTING: *Painted on a window we see (written backwards) "Quincy Flight School and FBO. M. L. Quincy, Prop." The office is cluttered with airplane pieces and a lot of paper. Walls are decorated with old pictures of airplanes and new photographs of theatre productions and actors. There are several large posters advertising theatrical productions. A computer sits on the desk.*

AT RISE: *Early morning. SOUND: A one-engine plane passes low overhead. Securely tied to a chair is SWASH BUNKER. He is gagged. SWASH wears an expensive World War II leather flying jacket complete with a white scarf around his neck.*

MARY LOU QUINCY is moving a floor lamp so it aims at SWASH's eyes. There already is a desk lamp shining in his face. MARY LOU is slim, vigorous, energetic, attractive. She moves and speaks in a staccato rhythm.

HECTOR CUNNINGHAM, dressed in mechanic's overalls, watches MARY LOU.

HECTOR
(Doubtfully.)

Somehow don't seem right, Mary Lou, ropin' down that there tourist.

SWASH
(Through the gag.)

Ummmm mmm MM! (Let me GO!)

MARY LOU

What I've got here, Hector, is the Holy Grail.

SWASH

UmmmMMM?! (What?!)

HECTOR
(Studying SWASH.)

Don't look all that holy to me.

MARY LOU

All right. Then what I've got here is Jason. The same Jason who got the Golden Fleece. What I want is a piece of it.

SWASH

Ummmhmmmm. Mmm MMMM! (Oh God. She's nuts!)

HECTOR

Mary Lou, I swear . . .

MARY LOU
(To SWASH.)

I knew you right away, soon as I saw the name on your plane.

SWASH

Ummmmm? (What?)

HECTOR

What name?

(HECTOR goes to the window and looks out.)

MARY LOU

"The Swashbuckler."

(To HECTOR.)

Isn't that what it says on the side of the plane?

HECTOR
(Spelling it out.)

S – W – A –

MARY LOU
(To SWASH.)
And you're Mr. Swash Bunker.

HECTOR
S – H – B – U – C – K –

MARY LOU
And now you're mine!

SWASH
Ummmmm. (Oh, Lord.)

HECTOR
L – E – R. That's Swashbum—Swashluck—

MARY LOU
Swash Buckler!

HECTOR
(Trying to understand.)
Didn't you say his name was Swash Bunker?

MARY LOU
(Patting SWASH's cheek.)
My own Jason.

SWASH
Mmm mm mm. (Don't touch me.)

HECTOR
Jason?

MARY LOU
With the Golden Fleece. That's what he's going to give me. Aren't
you?

SWASH
Hmmm, hhh MMM! (Lady, you're nuts.)

MARY LOU
(To HECTOR.)
Turn on that switch.

HECTOR
(Going to the switch.)
I swear I don't understand you sometimes. This poor guy flies in to
get gas. Lands out there. Comes in here. You tie him up.

MARY LOU
(Straining to be polite.)
The lights?

HECTOR
Because his name is Swash somethin' or other. Or Jason. Or Fleece.

MARY LOU
(As before.)
Please, Hector?

HECTOR
Like he's the sheep that lays the golden eggs?

(Thinking.)
Sheep? Naw. The chicken that lays . . . No, the . . .

MARY LOU
Hector: LIGHTS ON!

HECTOR
(A bit surprised. Blinking.)
Oh. Right

(HECTOR turns on the switch. The floor
lamp goes on. SWASH recoils from the

bright light. Both lights are intense, like an interrogation scene.)

SWASH

MMMmmm! (Hey!)

MARY LOU
(Thoughtfully.)
I wonder if we need a rubber hose.

HECTOR
(Delighted.)
Like them cop movies? For to hit him with?

(Almost dancing with delight.)
Violence! Violence!

SWASH

Umm Mmm! (No! No!)

MARY LOU
(Pointing at a poster.)
That's your play, isn't it?

(Reading.)
"Produced by Swash Bunker."

(Points at another poster.)
And that one. "This play produced by Swash Bunker."

(Picks up a copy of *Variety*.)
"Swash Bunker Production Tops Ten Mill." Oh, you're a busy producer, aren't you? But too busy for really talented writers, huh?

HECTOR
(Awed.)
Ten mill, like . . . like in *ten mill*?

MARY LOU
(Smiling gently at SWASH; the
Southern belle.)
And here you are. Dropped in for tea? How nice. How exquisitely,
lovely, perfectly nice. We all, Swash-baby, are goin' to have a party
with you all.

SWASH
Ummm? Ummmm. (Party? Ohhh.)

MARY LOU
I do hope ever so much you remember li'l ol' me. Mary Lou
Quincy? Playwright? Author of *Tomorrow and Tomorrow*? We'll
just have to talk about what you said about my play. Oooo, what
horrible, nasty things. But here you are! Land's sake, Swash-honey,
ain't Fate a son of a bitch?

SWASH
Mmm-mmm. (Oh-oh.)

HECTOR
(Awed.)
This guy's the one you sent your play to? The one who said you
oughta burn your typewriter and take up knittin' 'n' cookin' 'n'
makin' kids?

MARY LOU
(Grim.)
The very one.

HECTOR
Whooo-EEE! Mister, sayin' somethin' like that to Mary Lou means
you gotta be flyin' on half a wing!

Mailing Your Script

There are two rules regarding giving your play to others. The first is simple: Never let anyone see your play until you are convinced it is as perfect as you can make it. The second rule is even simpler: There are no exceptions to rule number one. A playwright is understandably eager to mail his or her script the moment it is finished, but that eagerness can damage the reputation of a writer who sends a script that can be improved.

Snail Mail or Email?

Many producing organizations prefer to receive electronic copies of scripts rather than hard copies. Before sending your script off, check the organization's submission expectations on its Call for Scripts or its Website. If you email your script as an attachment, turn it into a PDF document before sending it off unless the submission directions specify otherwise.

Mailing Envelopes and Mail-Worn Scripts

If you send your script using the postal service, some experts recommend that you protect its appearance by mailing it in a padded envelope. The idea makes sense because you don't want to send out mail-worn scripts that suggest they've been rejected many times.

Self-Addressed Stamped Envelope

Always include a self-addressed stamped envelope (SASE) when you mail your play. Otherwise it will not be returned to you, and most likely your script simply will be discarded. Worse, it may not even be read: Some producers, directors, publishers, and agents believe that the lack of an enclosed SASE indicates that the writer has an unprofessional attitude. Again, check the organization's submission expectations; some will indicate up front that they simply recycle unwanted scripts and will not use SASEs.

Self-addressed postcard.   You may wish to include a self-addressed, stamped postcard that the recipient can use to acknowledge receipt of the script. Type a simple message such as "We have received your play, *TOMORROW IS TOO LATE,*" and leave room for signature and date. If you're lucky, the recipient may write a brief note indicating when you can expect to receive notice about the fate of your play.

NOW GO FOR IT!

You've written the best play in your capabilities. Now be sure you package and send it in a manner that befits its quality.

11

Resources for the Playwright

> *Given the same natural qualifications, he who feels the emotions to be described will be the most convincing; distress and anger, for instance, are portrayed most truthfully by one who is feeling them at the moment. Hence it is that [playwriting] demands a man with a special gift for it, or else one with a touch of madness in him. The former can easily assume the required mood, and the latter may be actually beside himself with emotion.*
>
> — ARISTOTLE

"A touch of madness" can be valuable while you're writing, as Aristotle suggests in his *Poetics*: the moderately (or perhaps not so moderately) eccentric writer at work, busily talking to invisible characters, gesturing wildly with them as they battle unseen foes, laughing as they relish victories, or crying with their defeats. Relatives and neighbors walk quickly away, looking back over their shoulders at the Strange One. That sort of madness can even be enjoyable.

Unfortunately, however, lunacy also infects the business end of playwriting, and many playwrights are perplexed by the complex process—copyrighting your plays, getting an agent, finding details about contests and workshops, and locating directors and producers interested in new plays.

An apparent Catch-22 adds to the feeling that theatre is a mad, mad world. Some producers won't consider your play for professional production unless it is submitted by an agent, but many agents won't look at a beginner's work until the playwright has been produced, preferably professionally. More confusing, some play publishers recommend that playwrights explore the rich regional theatre market, but they also say that the best way to get their attention is with a successful production in Manhattan.

Although these circuitous denials appear confusing, they aren't brick walls. In the following pages we look at bright rays of sanity—various resources for the playwright—that can help you find a path through the confusing maze of the business end of playwriting.

Space limitations here prevent complete discussion of all possibilities (entire books are written on these subjects), so in this chapter we look at essential resources, give you basic information, and tell you where you can find additional information. More important, there are constant changes in business procedures, contractual forms, theatrical contests, workshops, organizations, and theatres and producers interested in new plays. Here we show you how and where to find the most recent information.

Organizations for Playwrights

Various national and local organizations for playwrights will give you valuable information and advice about contracts, royalties, agents, grants, contests, workshops, seminars, and theatres interested in new plays. Three of the more important organizations are described below.

Dramatists Guild

The Dramatists Guild, created in 1926 by 131 playwrights and originally called the Association of Dramatists, has grown into the primary organization for playwrights, lyricists, and composers, with more than 7,000 members. One of two divisions of the Authors League of America, Inc. (the other is the Authors Guild for book and magazine writers), the Dramatists Guild's numerous professional services deserve the attention of playwrights. If you are serious about being a playwright, you should be a Guild member.

Publications. The Guild publishes its journal *The Dramatist* (seven issues annually), "the only national magazine devoted to the business and craft of writing for theatre." It also publishes the annual *Dramatists Guild Resource Directory,* which lists career development professionals such as agents, development opportunities such as colonies and residencies, production possibilities such as contests and theatres that produce new plays, educational opportunities including workshops, writer resources, like books and software, and samples of submission letters, resumes, script formats, etc. Both *The Dramatist* and the *Resource Directory* are available to members in print form as well as on the Guild's website (dramatistsguild.com).

Dramatists Guild contracts. Guild members receive valuable support and advice regarding a wide variety of contractual arrangements. The Guild provides sample contracts for musicals, plays, small theatre premieres, collaborative work, commissioned scripts, and securing of under-lying rights for adaptations. These contracts set the theatrical standard for professional production, protecting playwrights in such matters as royal-ties, the writer's rights in his or her work, and disputes with producers.

Special services. The Guild offers advice about contracts, options, copyrights, taxes, and dealings with producers and agents. It also spon-sors seminars and workshops on various business and creative aspects of writing and holds occasional national conferences. Most areas of the country have regional Guild representatives who schedule local confer-ences and events. Members have access to the Guild's reference library, health plan, free ticket programs, and many other services.

Membership. Two categories of Guild membership are based on the playwright's writing experience. To be a Full Member, the playwright must have had a play produced before a paying audience or published by a recognizable publishing or licensing company. Associate Members must have written at least one play. Students receive substantial discounts on annual membership fees for both membership categories. See the Guild website for membership rates, discounts, and lists of benefits.

Address, telephone, & email. 1501 Broadway, Suite 701, New York, NY 10036; (212) 398 9366. info@dramatistsguild.com.

Theatre Communications Group (TCG)

In the 1950s, stimulated by an increasing desire to decentralize the-atre and made possible by governmental support and the Ford Founda-tion's multimillion-dollar grants program, there was a rapid growth of resident nonprofit professional theatres across the nation. The struggles of those regional theatres to survive led to the establishment of the The-atre Communications Group (TCG) in 1961, also funded by the Ford Foundation. TCG supports regional theatres, provides valuable services to playwrights, and actively encourages production of new plays.

Publications. TCG publishes the monthly *American Theatre*, often containing new plays; *Individual Member Wire*, an emailed newsletter for members; *Art SEARCH*, a bulletin of job opportunities in theatre; and numerous other publications.

Membership benefits. In addition to access to the publications listed above, individual TCG members receive a number of benefits including book discounts and online resources. For details, consult the website at tcg.org. However, possibly the most important benefit of membership is simply keeping informed about the network of professional theatres responsible for many productions of original plays across the country.

Address and telephone. 520 Eighth Avenue, 24th Floor, New York, NY 10018-4156; (212) 609-5901.

Playwrights' Center

Founded in 1971 by five writers seeking artistic and professional support, the Playwrights' Center today has a membership of some 2,000 playwrights around the world. The Center has been instrumental in launching the careers of many well-known playwrights including August Wilson, Lee Blessing, Suzan-Lori Parks, Craig Lucas, and Jeffrey Hatcher.

Services. Playwrights' Center membership is open to all. Center members can enjoy a large number of benefits including a comprehensive, curated database of playwriting opportunities, script feedback and dramaturgical assistance, and seminars and workshops from one-nighters to multiweek classes that are available in residence or online. The Core Writer program provides a deep level of support to 25–30 playwrights each year with play development workshops and assistance building relationships with producing theatres. Fellowship programs award more than $315,000 each year in partnership with funders such as the McKnight Foundation and the Jerome Foundation as well as a personalized array of services—workshops, dramaturgy, access to collaborators, professional connections—that is career-changing for most playwrights. Additionally, the Center has a New Plays on Campus program for colleges and universities designed to help jump-start the careers of the next generation of playwrights.

A strong service center with a long, successful track record, the Playwrights' Center is worth checking out.

Address, telephone, and website. 2301 E. Franklin Ave., Minneapolis, MN 55406. (612) 332-7481. Pwcenter.org

Local Playwrights' Associations

Dramatists' organizations are dedicated to the premise that playwrights can help one another by sharing insight, experience, and play critiques. You'll find strong playwrights' associations affiliated with regional theatres that offer playwrights opportunities for special readings or productions. Other groups may be part of state or regional writers' organizations.

You may enjoy the camaraderie of a writers' club with its opportunity to share interests with like-minded people and be part of a mutual support group. Some clubs are primarily social groups, made up of writers who can charitably be called hobbyists. Others show a more serious purpose, sponsoring play readings, contests, seminars with theatre professionals, and script-in-hand or workshop productions. Such organizations can help you make valuable contacts with producers, directors, agents, and publishers.

Locating a writers' organization in your area.   Your local theatrical organizations, the reference librarian at your town's library, or your local bookstore may have information about nearby writers' groups. Also search the Web for writing groups. Or start your own playwrights organization. You can gather other playwrights to form a dramatists group that meets in someone's home perhaps once a month for play readings and critiques. Establish working relationships with local theatres so your group can recruit actors to do script-in-hand readings of new plays and invite directors or other theatre experts to participate in critique sessions. As your plays improve, persuade your local theatres to sponsor workshop readings to invited audiences; from such informal beginnings have sprung a number of significant workshops.

Copyright

Beginning playwrights often are overly concerned about copyrighting their works to protect against misuse or outright theft, and even experienced playwrights are uncertain about what copyright actually means. As the creator of a play, you have certain legal ownership protections without going through the formal copyright registration process, and at any rate a copyright doesn't prevent an unscrupulous director or theatrical company from producing your play without obtaining your permission or paying royalties. Unfortunately, a few dishonest theatres do present plays without paying royalties, but these usually are small-fry producers whose lack of ethics probably extends in other areas that will result in their ultimate collapse.

What Is a Copyright?

Copyright is proof of ownership. When you buy a car you register it with your state's department of motor vehicles, receiving a certificate you can use to prove ownership. Equally, a copyright is an international "proof of ownership," showing that you registered your play with the U. S. Copyright Office. Just as your car's title does not mean the state guarantees your car will not be stolen or damaged, a copyright does not mean the Copyright Office, or any other agency of the United States government, will prosecute anyone suspected of misappropriating your work.

Advantages of Copyrighting Your Play

Registering your play's copyright gives you grounds for legal actions that you may wish to initiate if your play is produced or published without your permission. Copyright registration carries substantial legal benefits, and in a worst-case scenario when you have to resort to the courts, copyright registration is considered prima facie evidence. It also gives you legal standing to take actions to stop a misinterpreted production of your play. Samuel Beckett, for example, used copyright registration to stop an all-female production of *Waiting for Godot*. He said that if he had meant it to be done with an all-female cast, he would have written it that way, and he wouldn't permit a wrong-headed director to misinterpret the play.

Experts suggest that the relatively small fee for copyrighting a work is cheap because it gives the playwright the best legal protection available.

Not Eligible for Copyright

Copyright protection does not extend to everything you write. For example, you cannot copyright ideas or titles. More specifically, the United States Copyright Office says the following cannot be copyrighted: "Works that have not been fixed in a tangible form of expression. For example: choreographic works which have not been notated or recorded, or improvisational speeches or performances that have not been written or recorded. Titles, names, short phrases, and slogans; familiar symbols or designs; mere listings of ingredients of contents. Ideas, procedures, methods, systems, processes, concepts, principles, discoveries, or devices, as distinguished from a description, explanation, or illustration. Works consisting entirely of information that is common property and containing no original authorship."

Copyrighting Plays

You can copyright manuscripts of plays and even scenarios, but few playwrights bother to register scenarios because copyright protection is not extended to plays written from them. The Copyright Office defines this category as "published and unpublished works prepared for the purpose of being 'performed' before an audience or indirectly 'by means of any device or process.' Examples of works of the performing arts are: music works, including any accompanying words; dramatic works, including any accompanying music; pantomimes and choreographic works; and motion picture and other audiovisual works."

The Copyright Process

Forms and fees. Copyrighting your play is a relatively simple process. You fill out a form, obtainable for free from the Copyright Office (see address below), and return it with a copy of your play (or two copies if it is published) and the copyright fee. The Copyright Office then files your manuscript in its permanent archives and sends you a certificate proving you registered your play. Some playwrights frame the certificates for display in their offices; others store them with important papers for their heirs.

Marking the title page. It's a good idea to indicate to readers that your play is copyrighted by placing on the title page a statement such as: "Copyright (c) 2018 by J. T. Playwright." Better, use the international copyright symbol consisting of a circle around the letter C. You can draw the circle by hand. Some playwrights discourage potential thieves by putting the copyright notice on plays that aren't officially registered with the Copyright Office; the Copyright Office disapproves of this practice, and the lack of official registration eliminates some legal protections.

Publication. You need do nothing if your script is published by one of the play-publishing companies, such as Samuel French and Dramatists Play Service—they will copyright your play. Be sure the copyright is in your name, not the publisher's. Some experts point out, however, that your play may be in the marketplace for some time before it is accepted for publication, which suggests that you're better protected if you copyright your play before placing it in the mail.

Copyright Forms

The Copyright Office will send you necessary forms; to copyright your play, request *Application Form PA (Works of Performing Arts).*

Address, telephone, and website. Register of Copyrights, Copyright Office, Library of Congress, Washington, D.C. 20559. The Copyright Office Public Information Office phone number is (202) 707-3000. You will most likely find the answers to your questions on the Copyright Office's website—copyright.gov.

For Further Information

Here are three books that cover copyright details as well as other aspects of the business of playwriting:

Amada, Richard. *An Artist's Guide to the Law: Law & Legal Concepts Every Artist, Performer, Writer, or Other Creative Person Ought to Know.* Focus, 2010. Written by a lawyer who is also a playwright and TV journalist.

Bunnin, Brad, and Peter Beren. *The Writer's Legal Companion: The Complete Handbook for the Working Writer.* 3rd ed. Basic Books, 1998. An old standard.

Singer, Dana. *Stage Writers Handbook: A Complete Business Guide for Playwrights, Composers, Lyricists, and Librettists.* Theatre Communications Group, 1997. Written by an Associate Director of Dramatists Guild with a background in litigation who has worked on the staffs of Broadcast Music Inc. (BMI) and the Agency for the Performing Arts.

Additionally, current information about copyright can be found on the Dramatists Guild website. Because copyright law is modified from time to time, sources like the Guild's website that can be up-dated frequently may be more dependable than printed books that can become dated.

Literary Agents

Leaders of playwriting workshops and seminars report that the question they encounter most often is not, "What should I do to improve my playwriting?" but, "How do I get an agent?" The former question has to be answered before the latter: Despite some writers' expectations and hopes, a literary agent cannot jump-start a playwright's career. Agents—more properly, "authors' representatives"—believe you are not ready for representation until you have developed skills, typically through productions in amateur, professional, regional, or off- and off-off-Broadway theatres.

What Will an Agent Do?

Your special talent is writing plays; the agent's special talent is knowing the market. Expect a good agent to know precisely which New York or regional theatre producer or director is interested in what particular type of play, and to be familiar with foreign markets for your play. The agent submits your play scripts, handles complex business arrangements, represents you, negotiates contracts, insures your rights are protected so you are treated fairly, makes financial deals in your best interests, and attempts to find solutions to artistic conflicts that may arise. The agent also represents you in movie or television rights and publication. Many good agents will suggest revisions, but they are not playwriting teachers.

The Agent's Economics

The agent receives a certain agreed-upon percentage of the income you receive from scripts he or she handles, usually 10 percent but possibly up to 15 percent, and sometimes up to 20 percent for amateur rights. If your annual playwriting income is, say, $5,000, the agent's percentage would be $500 to $750. That would go toward paying agency salaries, overhead, telephone and fax bills, postage, and other expenses, hardly a profitable proposition for the agent. It is no wonder they look for playwrights with an established track record.

When Do You Need an Agent? And When Will an Agent Be Interested in Representing You?

You may want an agent after you have established a production record or have potential for a major production in New York or at a professional regional theatre, or when you have won a major national contest or are recommended by outstanding theatre experts. Agents interested in finding new writing talent may attend playwriting workshop readings or productions.

Agents urge clients to make their own contacts with those working in theatre, primarily directors and producers but certainly actors, designers, and others. Remember that the theatre world is small and overlapping: A director who presents your play at one theatre may move to a different one and recommend you for another production. Most directors and producers feel they have an obligation to replenish the font of theatre literature and are always looking for exciting new plays and new playwrights, and they enjoy discovering a writer and knowing they helped the playwright up the ladder.

Contacting an Agent

Agents get testy if you telephone or send unsolicited scripts. A more professional initial approach is a brief (one page maximum) query letter that introduces you, describes your writing and production highlights, indicates your future playwriting plans, and asks if you can send your latest script. Enclose a short (again, one page) description of your play and be sure to include a self-addressed stamped envelope with your query.

How many agents should you contact at the same time? There's no satisfactory answer. Some agents dislike being one of several you contact, but their all-too-common delay in replying makes that attitude seem unfair. You might have to wait several months for an answer; if that response is negative, then you must go through the inefficient query-and-wait process all over again. You'll have to decide whether to respect agents' wishes or follow your best interests.

A fair procedure is to query a number of agents, describing your play and its production history. If more than one requests the playscript, give all agents reading the script a reasonable opportunity to respond. If one expresses a strong interest, let other agents know so they can show their interest or return the script.

Advertisements for Critical Services

Beware of advertisements for critical services that imply they will serve as your agent if your script is "good enough." To make your script meet that nebulous standard, they'll offer to critique your play, but for a hefty fee. Too often the criticism will not be very helpful and you won't receive the agency representation you seek.

Although a reading fee does not by itself awaken suspicion, some self-proclaimed agents earn more from reading fees than from representing clients—hardly the service you need. Look at such offers with a healthy skepticism and decide if your money will be better spent in a good college playwriting course or at a workshop or seminar.

Contests, Workshops, Seminars, and Conferences

Several hundred organizations, dedicated to helping playwrights develop their plays, sponsor contests, workshops, seminars, and conferences. These give you valuable opportunities to meet theatre directors, producers, agents, and other playwrights and to establish contacts that can help you in the future.

Submission Requirements

Well before announced deadlines, write for application forms, rules, eligibility requirements, and other details. Enclose a self-addressed stamped envelope. Read specifications carefully; there's no point in sending a play that sponsors will not consider.

For further information regarding contests, workshops, and the like, obtain the *Dramatists Guild Resource Directory* or consult the Playwrights' Center's listing of opportunities.

Contests and Prizes

A number of playwriting contests are open each year, giving you opportunities for prizes, production, or publication, and frequently a combination of cash awards and production. Winners of contests involving production sometimes receive stipends for travel, room, and board so they can attend rehearsals of their plays. Again, utilize Dramatists Guild and Playwrights' Center listings to find contests.

Suggestions. Speaking as judges of contests that have drawn several hundred plays, we urge you to remember that judges are forced to look for reasons to eliminate the majority of the entries. Therefore you should carefully type your manuscript in standard playwriting format. Never send a script with misspellings, typos, or grammatical errors (unless they depict the character). Neatness is important. It's good strategy to enter your play well before the deadline to give readers a chance to study it before they are deluged with entries. Depending on submission specifications, consider including a concise (one or two paragraphs) synopsis of the play but avoid hypercute descriptions: "A hilarious modern comedy–tragedy in a new–old Greek–French classic style that the playwright's friends loved and you will, too" is guaranteed to put your play, unread, at the bottom of the pile.

Read rules carefully. Some contests are open to any entry. Others specify the type of play they'll accept, such as one-acts, full-lengths, musicals, translations, or plays for young audiences. Contests occasionally search for plays dealing with certain themes, defined in annual announcements (yet another reason to obtain contest rules well in advance).

Advantages in entering contests. Cash awards are attractive, but there are other reasons to enter contests. Prestigious contests draw attention to you and your work, opening possibilities of future productions, and there's a chance a contest judge may find your play attractive for his or her theatrical organization.

If you don't win. Rejections *will* come. Don't let them get you down. Contests may have three or five judges, and experience indicates that "winners" seldom are any single judge's first choice but instead are selected by a mathematical averaging system, which means first prize might go to a play that no judge ranked very highly. Each judge may have selected a different "first place" script, yet under the averaging system those plays might not receive even honorable mention, and you may not even know that your play was high on one judge's list. If you have faith in your play, react to rejections by entering it in other contests.

Workshops and Conferences

Numerous new play workshops and conferences in various parts of the country are dedicated to developing playwrights and playscripts, sometimes providing stipends for room, board, and travel to the site. These are valuable experiences, well worth your consideration.

While each workshop has different goals and operations, most require that you have at least one completed script to be studied and revised while you're in residence for several weeks, often during the summer, working closely with playwrights, directors, actors, or critics. Most put your play on its feet in a staged reading. Discussions identify your play's strengths and weaknesses, and you receive suggestions for revisions. You also will make valuable contacts with potential producers, directors, and agents. Again, listings from the Dramatists Guild and Playwrights' Center can help you identify these residencies.

Productions

Playwrights may dream of a star-studded Broadway performance that brings fame and fortune, but an examination of Broadway's offerings leads one to the conclusion that today's producers seldom favor new plays and are even less interested in unknown playwrights.

Alternatives to Broadway

If Broadway closes itself off to new plays, however, an active theatrical decentralization process opens numerous other production possibilities that deserve your attention. Many off- and off-off-Broadway organizations, as well as regional theatres across the country, are dedicated to new playwrights and have given now well-known playwrights their start. You also can receive excellent productions in community and college theatres. These experiences can build your morale, give you motivation to continue writing, and help you improve your plays.

Off- and Off-Off-Broadway

Off-Broadway. Off-Broadway began, if a date can be attached to a movement that did not instantly spring full-grown into existence, in 1952 with Jose Quintero's production of Tennessee Williams's poetic drama of loneliness, *Summer and Smoke*, presented at the Circle in the Square in Greenwich Village. At least that was the first non-Broadway show to receive a major review in the *New York Times*, legitimizing a movement that offered a lively alternative to the increasingly stale Broadway fare.

Despite popular opinion, off-Broadway is not a geographic region in Manhattan but is more an economic arrangement between producers and theatrical unions, based on the number of seats available for sale. Unions such as Actors Equity, which sets salaries for professional actors, agreed to establish a lower pay scale for auditoriums with a seating capacity of 499 or fewer (off-Broadway) than the standard higher scale for houses with 500 or more (Broadway). Typical off-Broadway theatres seat fewer than 200 people. The agreement frees professional actors to perform in low-budget off-Broadway shows. In Manhattan, there are more of the small-size auditoriums than the large, thus more off-Broadway houses and, by extension, more theatrical productions that use the abundant talent pool of actors, directors, designers, and technicians. And—important for you—more opportunities to have your play produced in New York.

Through the 1950s and into the 1960s, off-Broadway's advantage was its freedom from various theatrical unions' economic pressures for high salaries, coupled with visionary writers, directors, actors, and producers who wanted to create an alternative to Broadway's focus on slick commercial fare that neglected controversial or new ideas. Off-Broadway started on the proverbial shoestring, and many theatres mounted productions for less than $500, which meant they could be economically sound even with relatively small audiences. But theatre followed its normal hunger to grow, and by the end of the 1960s, production costs soared to over $15,000, requiring larger audiences, which in turn shifted focus to commercially promising plays. Off-Broadway began to look like Broadway's clone. Production costs now can range from $250,000 to $500,000, turning what was an iconoclastic free-spirited off-Broadway movement into a commercial organization like Broadway.

Off-Off-Broadway. Logically, then, off-off-Broadway was born. Prompted by the same vision that started off-Broadway, and with major concessions from unions such as Actors Equity, the movement again is a factor of the maximum number of auditorium seats—in this case, no more than 99 seats. Off-off-Broadway theatre means churches, lofts, basements, and warehouses. Small theatres sprang up, as many as 150 at one time. Chief among them was La Mama, founded in 1961 by Ellen Stewart, which presented a large number of plays and gave a hearing to many new playwrights such as Sam Shepard. Representative contemporary playwrights who received their start in off-off-Broadway include Spalding Gray, author of the monodrama *Swimming to Cambodia,* and Lanford Wilson, known for one-acts such as *Ludlow Fair* and full-lengths such as *Talley's Folly.* Although they are low-budget and nonprofit organizations, off-off-Broadway theatres provide excellent opportunities for playwrights.

You'll find that off-off-Broadway is open to original plays, ranging from traditional realism to experimental or avant-garde, and that a strong core of producers, directors, and actors are eager to stage works by new playwrights. Some organizations, however, claim to be interested in original plays but are really interested in plays by their own staff members, and you will discover current attitudes only through persistent applications and queries.

Although making contacts is easier if you live in the area, at conferences and seminars you'll meet actors and directors who are eager to work off-off-Broadway and might be interested in your scripts.

Regional Theatres

As the decentralization process gave birth to off-Broadway, equally strong motivations started the regional theatre movement. Today there are more than three hundred not-for-profit professional regional theatres across the nation, bringing new excitement to our art.

Regional theatres, represented by such organizations as Arena Stage (Washington), Goodman Theatre (Chicago), Alley Theatre (Houston) and the Mark Taper Forum (Los Angeles), are known for their professionalism and excellence. Some, like the Yale Repertory Theatre and the Actors Theatre of Louisville, present annual new play festivals. Regional theatres also present workshop productions and readings of new plays in small studio theatres. Some regional theatres premiere new plays that ultimately become New York successes.

If you believe you have a stageworthy script, make personal contacts with the regional theatre nearest you. You may have to be persistent to catch the attention of directors and actors, but the end result can be an excellent production of your play.

A Do-It-Yourself Showcase Production

A showcase production is aptly named: It exhibits talent. Playwrights, actors, and directors frequently sponsor showcase productions in New York's off-off-Broadway theatres, using small auditoriums, keeping expenses to a minimum, perhaps financing the performances themselves or finding sponsors. The stage experience helps theatre artists develop their skills. Showcases also give them valuable exposure, and they make a special point of inviting critics, producers, directors, and agents.

Showcase productions aren't limited to New York residents. Even if you don't live in New York, you can put together an off-off-Broadway showcase production of your play, using actors and directors you've met through various seminars, conventions, and productions. If that isn't possible, by all means consider a showcase production in your local facilities such as a public library, community theatre, high school auditorium, coffeehouse, or the like, perhaps in association with your local dramatists club or community or university theatre. Invite local theatre experts to attend and discuss the production. The showcase puts your play on its feet in the crucible of audience response, thereby helping you improve your writing skills, and it can lead to subsequent productions.

Conclusion

One conclusion can be stated simply: Be persistent. You learn to improve your writing from seeing your plays in rehearsals and productions, which means you must think of yourself as your own sales expert, taking all possible steps to get your plays staged. Think of marketing as a do-it-yourself project—after all, a play sitting in your file cabinet can't get a production. Take advantage of the many options we've described. Be patient. While you're developing your skills, don't expect immediate professional production but instead find other avenues, including self-production in local showcases.

A second conclusion also is simple: Make contacts. Develop working relationships with playwrights, producers, directors, and actors. That isn't as distasteful as it may sound to those who believe their plays should speak for themselves. The theatrical world is a small, close-knit community, more supportive of its members than outsiders recognize, and theatre people you meet in one situation can recommend your plays in other environments. Be active in your local theatres. Attend workshops, seminars, and conferences. You'll meet interesting people and find a great deal of support.

Finally, don't be imprisoned by the "Broadway mentality." Of course playwrights dream of a Broadway production with a star-studded, superglitzy opening and the post-show party at a famed watering hole while waiting for the reviews. Broadway's legends and excitement are powerful attractions. We hope you make it there, but it is a mistake to expect your first play—or even your first half-dozen plays—to become part of the Broadway legend. First you must pay your dues, learning your art and craft through writing a number of plays, in effect serving an apprenticeship in an educational process no less important than that demanded of doctors and lawyers. Don't think that a Broadway production is the only measure of your success as a playwright. Instead think of production as your goal—production in your own town, in educational and community theatres, children's groups, religious organizations, and in regional theatres.

We started this chapter with a reference to "a touch of madness." It is appropriate to conclude the chapter, and this book, with a different tone:

> *Children, you must remember something. A man without ambition*
> *is dead. A man with ambition but no love is dead. A man with*
> *ambition and love for his blessings here on earth is ever so alive.*
> *Having been alive, it won't be hard in the end to lie down and rest.*
>
> — Pearl Bailey

Good luck and good writing!

Writers at Work
(Part Two)

STAN: We could be the greatest, Gene. The greatest comedy writers in
   America. . . . I just have to learn to deal with the pressure.
EUGENE: So do I. It's not easy for me either.
STAN: I'm feeling better. I'm glad we had this talk. It reassures me that
   you want to stick with me. I'm feeling more relaxed now.
EUGENE: So am I.
STAN: . . . Now if we can just get an idea.

NEIL SIMON
Broadway Bound

Index